La Vie est Belle

La Vie est Belle

The elegant art of living
in the French style

Henrietta Heald

RYLAND PETERS & SMALL
LONDON • NEW YORK

Designers Maria Lee-Warren,
Sonya Nathoo and Megan Smith
Commissioning editor Annabel Morgan
Location research Christina Borsi
Production manager Gary Hayes
Art director Leslie Harrington
Editorial director Julia Charles

First published in 2013
by Ryland Peters & Small
20–21 Jockey's Fields,
London WC1R 4BW
and
519 Broadway, 5th Floor
New York, NY 10012
www.rylandpeters.com

10 9 8 7 6 5 4 3 2 1

Text © Ryland Peters & Small 2013
with the exception of the recipes on
the following pages: 14, 28, 44, 78,
90, 98, 111, 122, 129 and 140
© Laura Washburn 2003; 153, 170
and 181 © Clare Ferguson 2007

Design and photography
© Ryland Peters & Small 2013

ISBN 978 1 84975 452 1
A catalogue record for this book is
available from the British Library.
US Library of Congress cataloging-in-
publication data has been applied for.
Printed and bound in China

Contents

Introduction

My love of France began in early childhood. I grew up in the south of England, and among my earliest memories are dawn car journeys to one of the Channel ports – Southampton or Newhaven – to catch the ferry to Cherbourg, Dieppe and other exotic-sounding places. In those days, we were destined for fashionable bucket-and-spade resorts such as Bénodet on the southern Brittany coast.

I returned recently to Bénodet, after a gap of many years, and it seemed that little had changed. Holiday homes and supermarkets had sprung up, of course, but the essential character of the place – with its small beachfront hotels and cafés, wide swathes of sand and weekly produce market – was easily recognizable. Indeed, a sense of permanence and continuity, and the way these qualities are valued, is one of the special things about France.

In my later teenage years I was drawn to the glamour of St Tropez and other hotspots on the Cote d'Azur, but I soon realized that the interior of France had just as much to offer as the coastlines – and that, from the Ardennes to the Pyrenees, there was an endless variety of places to discover.

Marriage into a family of Francophiles with a home near Chantilly, north of Paris, has meant that I have continued to visit France at least once a year – yet I still feel as if I have only scratched the surface of this fascinating land.

La Vie est Belle is a celebration of the best things about France, from its champagne to its cheeses. By focusing on five areas with their own strong character, each one popular with both the French themselves and visitors, it aims to extol the particular qualities of the country as a whole.

Each chapter contains a selection of classic recipes associated with the area in question. Also covered are aspects of history and customs, food and wine, architecture and interior design, including the flea markets of Paris, the wine-growing regions of Bordeaux and the origins of toiles de Jouy.

There is also a series of features on beautiful homes in each of the chosen regions. Including an artist's retreat in Burgundy, a restored chateau in the Luberon and an antique collector's home in Nîmes, all these properties have a distinctive identity that has been shaped and nurtured by its owner or owners. All the houses featured have something in common. Despite their individualist approach to interior design, the owners share a reverence for the past and a desire to preserve it for future generations. They also take delight in mixing old and new. When it comes to decoration and furnishings, as well as the fabric of buildings, *racines* – meaning roots, or provenance – are at the heart of everything.

Henrietta Heald

Une Coupe de Champagne

Paris and the North

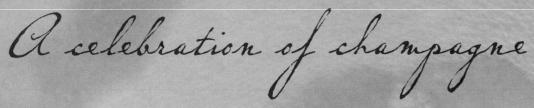

A celebration of champagne

Champagne is the supreme symbol of 'the good life', but it has surprisingly modest roots, originating in France's northernmost vineyards, near the cities of Reims and Epernay, 150 km (90 miles) north-east of Paris. Despite its thin clay soil and cool climate, the Champagne region provides the environment in which the classic sparkling-wine grapes of Chardonnay, Pinot Noir and Pinot Meunier achieve their finest expression.

The cool conditions here intensify the grapes' flavours while maintaining their acidity and freshness. Above all, the region has a distinctive chalky subsoil, which conserves moisture for the vines and adds a special mineral character to the grapes.

Genuine champagne is made by the *méthode traditionelle*. After fermentation, the wines – which may be from different vintages, vineyards and grapes – are blended together. Before bottling, a solution of yeast, sugar and wine is added, causing a second fermentation in the bottle, which produces the bubbles.

Sealed with crown caps, the bottles mature on their sides for up to three years, after which they are regularly shaken and upended so that the sediment moves down to the neck of the bottle. The neck is frozen and, when the cap is removed, the icy pellet of sediment is forced out by the pressure of the fizzy wine.

The bottle is topped up with a wine and sugar solution, sealed with a champagne cork and secured with a wire muzzle. It is left to mature for a further three to six months before being labelled and put on sale.

The region has a distinctive chalky subsoil, which adds a special mineral character to the grapes.

13

French onion soup, topped with toasted baguette slices and bubbling Gruyère cheese, is the perfect winter warmer, but it is also associated with traditional ritual. At French weddings, especially country weddings, it was often served in the early hours of the morning as a restorative after a whole night of celebrations. Long, slow cooking in butter and oil followed by gentle simmering in stock allows the rich flavour of the onions to develop to the full.

Soupe gratinée à l'oignon

50 g/3½ tablespoons
  unsalted butter
1 tablespoon olive oil
3 large onions, about
  1.3 kg/3 lbs., thinly sliced
2 garlic cloves, crushed
1 tablespoon plain/
  all-purpose flour
1 litre/4 cups beef, chicken
  or vegetable stock
600 ml/2½ cups dry
  white wine
1 fresh bay leaf
2 sprigs of thyme
1 baguette, sliced
about 180 g/1½ cups finely
  grated Gruyère cheese
coarse sea salt and freshly
  ground black pepper

Serves 4–6

Put the butter and oil in a large saucepan and melt over medium heat. Add the onions and cook over low heat for 15–20 minutes, until soft and transparent.

Add the garlic and flour and cook, stirring, for about 1 minute. Add the stock, wine, bay leaf and thyme. Season with salt and pepper and bring to the boil. Boil for 1 minute, then lower the heat and simmer very gently for 20 minutes.

Taste and adjust the seasoning. At this point, the soup will be cooked, but standing time will improve the flavour – at least 30 minutes.

Before serving, preheat the grill/broiler. Put the baguette slices on a baking sheet and brown under the grill/broiler until lightly toasted. Set aside. Do not turn the grill/broiler off.

To serve, ladle the soup into ovenproof bowls and top with a few toasted baguette rounds. Sprinkle grated cheese over the top and cook under the still-hot grill/broiler until browned and bubbling. Serve immediately.

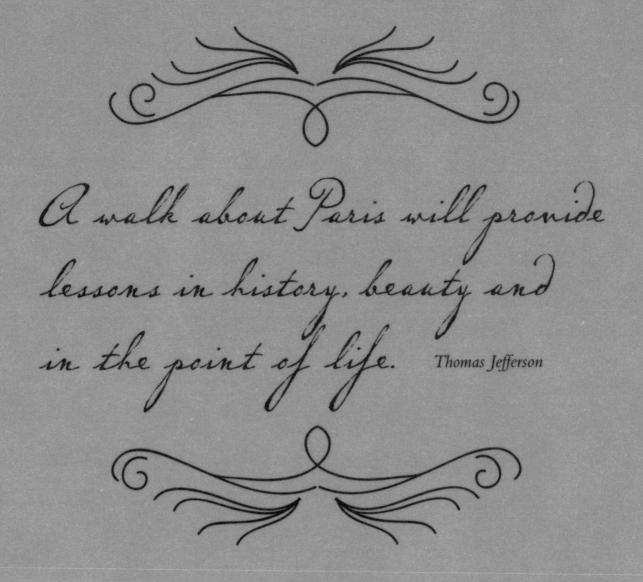

A walk about Paris will provide lessons in history, beauty and in the point of life. Thomas Jefferson

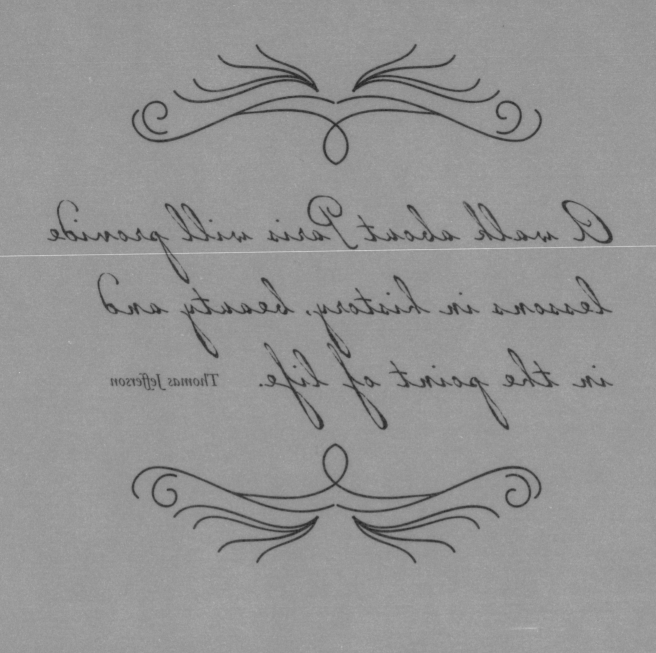

An artist's retreat

From the moment you walk through the door of Claire Basler's home in Burgundy, it is obvious that you are in the presence of a prolific and highly talented artist – an artist who is inspired particularly by the natural world. Indeed, it was a love of nature that first drew Claire to this house as a weekend retreat in 2005. At the time, she was living and working in Montreuil, a suburb of Paris, but had long dreamed of moving to the countryside. Four years later, it became her permanent home.

The house is in the village of Les Ormes in northern Burgundy, part of an area of farmland and forests called Puisaye, renowned for its tranquil beauty, but nevertheless only 1½ hours away from Paris. This was an important consideration for Claire, who likes to stay in close contact with the Paris art world. She shares the house with her partner, Pierre Imhof, two dogs and two cats; her three children have grown up and left home.

Dating from the 19th century, the three-storey building was once a convent school. Former classrooms have been converted into a living room, a dining room, an artist's studio and a library, but Claire did not change the proportions or layout of the interior. 'I kept the nuns' cells,' she says, 'and the large students' dormitory became my bedroom.' The former dormitory is dominated by a canopy bed with a metal frame but no cover, creating the impression of a room within a room. Behind it is a dramatic canvas of swirling browns and oranges suggesting dense woodland. The austerity of the plain wooden floor and the muted wall colours – here and elsewhere in the house – makes an ideal backdrop for the display of paintings.

When Claire took it over, the building had not been lived in for 50 years and a huge amount of work was necessary. The opening of a school in the village had forced the closure of the convent, and subsequent owners had not maintained the structure, so Claire had to go back to basics. Electricity, plumbing and central heating were installed. The windows, the shutters and some of the floors had to be replaced, as well as part of the roof. Most, but not all, of the walls were repainted. 'Some of them looked good left just as they were, in a rough, unimproved state,' says Claire. Each storey has an abundance of tall windows – and the light-filled interior makes it the perfect place for an artist.

OPPOSITE AND ABOVE RIGHT Canvases of silky white blooms against a dark background dominate the entrance hall. Dried flowerheads are used to make a quirky sculpture and displayed in bottles on the stairs, adding an informal note.

RIGHT The huge hanging cupboard was made out of old doors found in a *brocante* and renovated; above them is a smaller, matching cupboard with new plywood doors. The whole structure is painted to appear as if it were part of the wall.

The choice of decorative colours was influenced by the quality of the light in each part of the house.

Every space you enter has a surprise in store. On one wall of Claire's bedroom, for example, is a series of canvases of lilies, in blues and greys, a palette that the artist loves. Among the eclectic items of furniture in this room are some iron console tables made by her brother Jérôme, and a pair of glass display shelves from a baker's shop, which serve as bedside tables. Another, smaller bedroom – one of six in total – has walls of midnight blue and, at the head of the bed, a painting of anemones in colours that recall a storm at sea. Claire identifies the combination of strength and fragility seen in this canvas as one of the defining characteristics of her work.

Claire's studio is on the first floor. To her, this is the most important part of the building – a room so overflowing with fresh flowers that it's difficult to tell where nature ends

and art begins. 'I have always worked from home,' she explains, 'so, wherever I've lived, my studio has been part of the house.' She is equally attached to her garden, which is enclosed by high walls at the front and overlooks fields at the back. Its features include a row of old lime trees, an orchard area and a pond surrounded by wild flowers. Claire describes her garden as a source of inspiration that is quite distinct from untamed nature, especially when it comes to colours. 'The garden charms and seduces me, it brings me gifts,' she says. 'It is the continuity of the house. It is the image of happiness.'

ABOVE LEFT The original nuns' refectory-cum-kitchen has been divided into several smaller rooms. A painted screen of nine panels, each one 3 metres (10 feet) high, demarcates the formal dining area.

ABOVE RIGHT The distinctive star-tiled floor shows that this 'service area', used for storing plates and dishes, was once part of the convent refectory. Claire's two dogs, Prune and Ziza, have taken up residence there.

RIGHT The kitchen installed by Claire, where most meals are eaten, is traditional in style with a wonderful mixture of old and new elements. A particularly eye-catching modern piece is the lampshade above the table, which resembles the Pipistrello shade designed by the Italian architect Gae Aulenti. The black-and-yellow colour scheme was chosen to augment the effect of sunlight streaming through the window.

ABOVE AND RIGHT Everything is beautifully displayed. Fresh flowers stand to attention on the windowsill above the kitchen sink. Beside them, spoons, forks and kitchen implements are lined up in a row of old paint pots – all painted earthy red to create visual harmony.

LEFT AND OPPOSITE One wall in the main bedroom is graced with a series of lily paintings so luminous that they convey a sense of being under water. Claire can enjoy this effect while lying in bed on the other side of the room. **BELOW LEFT** The scale and arrangement of the spaces in this former convent create some intriguing vistas. **RIGHT** This guest bedroom is painted midnight blue, but its austerity is softened by the tints of pink and mauve in the canvas behind the bed. **BELOW** Even the bathroom benefits from Claire's artistic exuberance, which here takes the form of irises painted on a silver canvas.

Classic furniture

Antique furniture and lighting – often left unrestored, in the state in which is was found – is a feature of many French homes. Pride of place among France's classic furniture pieces is taken by the armoire – a freestanding wooden cupboard that looks at home in any room. In a kitchen or dining room it may store tableware, glass or cutlery/flatware. In a bedroom or bathroom its shelves may be piled high with linen or folded clothes. An armoire may be polished, painted or limewashed.

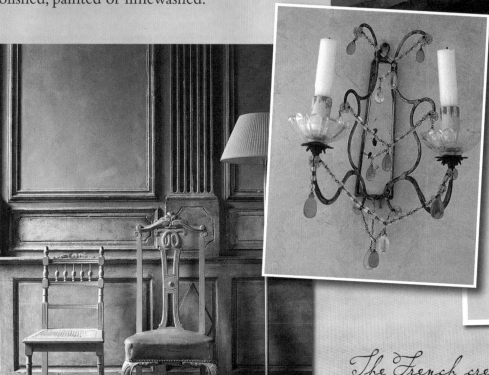

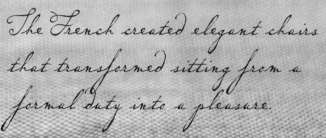

The French created elegant chairs that transformed sitting from a formal duty into a pleasure.

Related to the armoire is the smaller *garde à manger*, a lower cupboard with doors below open shelves, perhaps protected by a chicken-wire grille. Used for food storage, these pieces were hung from the ceiling or high on a wall. The *buffet*, or low cupboard, is another popular piece used for both storage and display. It sometimes has an upper tier that may be simply shelves, or may be another, smaller cupboard, when it is know as a *buffet à deux corps*.

Starting in the reign of Louis XV (1723–74), the French created a series of elegant chairs that transformed sitting from a formal duty into a pleasure. Originals and reproductions of these are still widely available. Among them are the *fauteuil*, a low-backed, feather-stuffed armchair; the *bergère*, a tub chair with upholstered arms and cushions; the *marquise*, a love seat; the *canapé*, an intimate sofa; and the *chaise longue*, a daybed.

When the influential American chef Julia Child first came to France in 1948, she was entranced by this simple but supremely satisfying French fish dish, which takes just a few minutes to cook. Indeed, her first taste was a culinary revelation. 'The flesh of the sole was delicate, with a light but distinct taste of the ocean that blended marvelously with the browned butter,' she wrote in her memoir *My Life in France*. 'It was a morsel of perfection.' This recipe is for a whole fish, but you can use fillets of sole instead and slightly reduce the cooking time.

Sole meunière

2–3 tablespoons plain/
   all-purpose flour
2 fresh sole, about 300 g/
   10 oz. each, skinned and
   cleaned
2 tablespoons sunflower/
   safflower oil
40 g/3 tablespoons unsalted
   butter
fine sea salt
freshly squeezed juice of
   half a lemon
a handful of flat-leaf
   parsley, finely chopped
lemon slices, to serve

Serves 2

Put the flour on a large plate, add the fish, cover with flour on both sides and shake off the excess.

Heat the oil and 1 tablespoon of the butter over medium-high heat in a non-stick frying pan large enough to hold both fish side by side. When it sizzles, add the sole and cook for about 3 minutes. Turn them over and cook on the other side for 3 minutes. Sprinkle the first side with salt while the second side is cooking.

When the fish are cooked through, transfer to warmed serving plates and season the second side.

Return the frying pan to the heat, add the remaining butter and melt over high heat. When it begins to sizzle, lower the heat and add the lemon juice. Cook, scraping the pan for about 10 seconds; do not let the butter burn. Pour the sauce over the fish and sprinkle with parsley. Serve immediately, garnished with thin slices of lemon.

A touch of glamour

Marina Coriasco is the art director of French *Glamour*, a Condé Nast magazine based in Paris. She and her husband, Arnaud de Fortis, moved to this apartment in south central Paris in 1998 from the more fashionable Marais district. They were looking for a child-friendly loft with a garden on the ground floor and they were drawn to this building, a former warehouse, because of its potential and its outdoor space. Another attraction was the proximity of the beautiful Parc Raspail.

OPPOSITE The industrial aesthetic of the former warehouse has been preserved, making a perfect setting for a mix of old and new. In the dining area, for example, an old farmhouse table is flanked by a set of Tolix A chairs and illuminated by an ornate crystal chandelier. A blown-up print from a Christian Dior advertising campaign dominates the space.
ABOVE LEFT AND RIGHT Tall bookshelves divide the open-plan living area into smaller spaces.
RIGHT A retro oriental poster, a vase of garden roses and a 1970s plastic ashtray create an arresting still life.

LEFT A 1970s sofa and a Gustavian chest of drawers are united by the soft colour scheme of white, greys and greens.
BELOW Upholstered in white linen, with a frame of slate grey, this capacious *bergère* chair has a contemporary feel, although it probably dates from the 18th century.

OPPOSITE Antique French furniture is combined with oriental and rustic details and jewel-like colours to create an individual look in this elegant bedroom, one of four in the apartment. The pictures and decorative items here and elsewhere were mostly picked up by Marina at markets and second-hand shops.

In transforming the warehouse into a comfortable home, Marina and Arnaud decided to retain the industrial aesthetic of the building. For example, they installed a prominent steel beam across the ceiling of the main living area, which looks as if it has always been there. In fact, the beam was just one element of a major building project. When Marina and Arnaud arrived, there were walls, a floor and a roof, and very little else. They were responsible for the entire remodelling of the interior, which covers 260 square metres (2,800 square feet).

Apart from other interests, Arnaud is a designer, builder and decorator, and between them the couple designed and made many things in their home – from windows and doors to tables and chairs. Wooden floors, mainly pine, were laid throughout, even in the two bathrooms, where they were sealed with a special paint.

One early venture was to install a huge window in the steeply pitched roof to allow light to flood into the main living space. There are Velux windows in three of the four bedrooms, and conventional windows in their son Eliot's room, which has a small balcony. The main bathroom is also full of light, which comes both from an exterior window and from a frosted window in the wall linking the bathroom with the open-plan living space.

Une Coupe de Champagne

RIGHT AND INSET
A minimalist window treatment blurs the boundary between inside and out, while the dainty hanging lantern is just one of many objects with an oriental theme.
BELOW Dominated by the vintage claw-foot bathtub, painted black for dramatic effect, the bathroom is full of natural light. The light comes from two sources – an ordinary window and a row of opaque-glass panels that separates the bathroom from the main living space.

The main living space encompasses some 80 square metres (860 square feet). Leading off it are two offices – one for Eliot, who is studying to be a designer, and one for Marina herself, who works at home one day a week so that she can spend time with her seven-year-old daughter, Daria. Although there is a separate dining room, the kitchen is large enough to include a table for informal meals.

Apart from the furniture made by Arnaud – such as the industrial-style chairs in the kitchen – many of the pieces in the apartment are vintage, acquired from markets or via eBay. The freestanding, claw-foot bathtub in the main bathroom is an original inherited from Arnaud's family. However, the distinctive three-seater sofa in the living room was bought from Merci, a market-style store in the Marais, which describes itself as 'Paris's latest concept shopping sensation'. And the classic Tolix A chairs in the dining room come from Le Bon Marché, Paris's oldest department store.

The kitchen leads straight out into the garden area, which is also accessible from the front entrance. The garden occupies 60 square metres (650 square feet), part of which is covered by decking and part by terracotta tiles. There is a set of wrought-iron chairs and table shaded by an ever-expanding vine – ideal for outdoor dining whenever the weather permits. An olive and a palm tree are among the plants that flourish in the deep terracotta pots.

LEFT AND INSET For Marina and Arnaud, one of the main attractions of this Paris apartment in the Cachan district was its charming, vine-shaded courtyard, where a mixture of decking, faded exterior panelling and old tiles creates a pleasantly rustic feel. Suspended from the branches of the vine are several Moroccan lanterns, which throw a dappled light on the wrought-iron table and chairs – scene of many a happy evening meal. Unusually for Paris, Cachan has a large number of private gardens and tree-filled public parks, including Parc Raspail, making it an ideal residential area for families with young children.

Marchés aux puces

Second-hand markets and antiques fairs are a well-established feature of French life, but none is more enduringly popular than the *marché aux puces* held every weekend at St-Ouen, Porte de Clignancourt, in Paris's 18th *arrondissement*. More than just a flea market, Les Puces is a consortium of flea markets, consisting of more than 3,000 stalls and shops selling everything from antique furniture and jewellery to clothing and bric-a-brac. Like Paris's two other great flea markets at Vanves and Montreuil, Les Puces can trace its origins back to the 18th century.

Even more spectacular is La Braderie, the annual flea market in Lille, where, during the first weekend in September, more than a million visitors descend to hunt for bargains on more than 10,000 stalls.

Thousands of second-hand markets on a more modest scale, called *brocantes*, can be found all over France. As well as offering a vivid insight into local life, a visit to a *brocante* almost always yields unusual items that you simply won't see in the shops. A *vide-grenier* – literally, an emptying of the attic – is the least formal type of market, resembling a yard sale in the US or a car-boot sale in the UK, where anyone can make a bit of cash from selling unwanted treasures.

An elegant showcase

Art galleries, vintage boutiques, restaurants and bars abound in the fashionable Marais district of Paris, which has enjoyed a major renovation and renaissance in recent years. Centred on the ancient place des Vosges – a perfect square – the Marais was once home to the Parisian aristocracy, who disappeared after the French Revolution. Today, having survived a long period of neglect, it has more pre-revolutionary buildings and streets left intact than any other area in Paris.

ABOVE This intriguing apartment in the Marais is not only a comfortable home but also a showcase for carefully chosen antiques. An amazing array of objects greets visitors at every turn. This display includes two large fossilized stones resembling human faces and a pair of chunky table lamps made from wooden staircase balustrades.

LEFT A cool pastel colour scheme has been chosen for the small bedroom, but the rich red velvet pillows on the bed add a note of warmth and drama. The panelled bedhead conceals a capacious double clothes cupboard.
OPPOSITE In winter, a curious pair of bellows incorporating a real tortoise shell are used to keep the fire burning in the living room.

LEFT AND ABOVE A floor-to-ceiling display cabinet covers one entire wall of the dining room. Visible behind the glazed doors in the top half of the cabinet is a variety of stuffed birds, juxtaposed with a seemingly random selection of ordinary and extraordinary objects, including a pinboard of colourful butterflies.

OPPOSITE Occupying centre stage is an 18th-century Swedish table flanked by four wooden chairs with leather seats. By contrast with these low-key objects, the pictures, mirrors and decorative items make a dramatic impact. Coral fronds seem to grow out of a pair of cast-iron garden urns.

Among the many entrepreneurs living and working in the Marais is the antiques dealer Franck Delmarcelle, who owns a shop called Galerie Et Caetera on the narrow rue de Poitou. Franck characterizes his collection as 'poor chic – objects that don't necessarily have an intrinsic value, but which have a soul'. Signs of a former life – cracks and blemishes, slightly torn or faded upholstery – all contribute to this sense of soul.

A similar aesthetic is evident in the apartment that Franck lives in with his partner Laurent Dombrowicz, just a few minutes' walk from the shop. Franck is also a skilled interior decorator who enjoys mixing and matching styles

and objects. He frequently invites clients to his home, which he treats as an exhibition space, a showcase for his work. Muted wall colours and floors covered in dark pine planks or well-worn tiles provide neutral backdrops. 'I wanted it to resemble houses in Holland, which often have black floors,' Franck explains.

The entrance hall is the first of seven rooms, each one leading off the next, all displaying an eclectic, sometimes startling choice of furniture. For example, the study contains a rustic table, an ornate painted desk, two Louis XV chairs and a daybed, to which Franck has attached an iron frame topped by a carved and gilded crown.

Both bizarre and beautiful, the decorative objects in the apartment include a stuffed Patagonian hare, collections of mercury glass and concrete toadstools. Stuffed creatures and religious iconography appear throughout. For Franck and Laurent, taxidermy allows the beauty of animals and birds to be appreciated after death. Similarly, their love of iconography reflects an appreciation of the craftsmanship and emotional investment that went into making the pieces, rather than any religious belief.

A row of tall cupboards with glazed upper doors occupies an entire wall in the dining room. On view inside, as well as more stuffed animals, are even more unusual collections – from pieces of coral, shells, butterflies and a giant cockroach carapace to a child's model Citroen from the 1950s that conceals an iPod dock. 'I like the idea of accumulation,' says Franck. The pale blue walls create an aura of calm refinement that perfectly complements the 18th-century Swedish dining table and chairs.

A subtle harmony is achieved in the salon between the brown-grey walls and the hexagonal terracotta tiles on the floor, polished by years of use. The roughly hewn shutters are made from reclaimed scaffolding boards, a surprising contrast to the upholstered sofas, while the use of garden statuary creates a pleasing link with the outdoors.

Clever use has been made of space in the bedroom, which is uncluttered and unadorned. Although the panelling behind the bed appears purely decorative, in fact it conceals a commodious set of fitted cupboards. Apart from the bed, the only other piece of furniture is a long cane seat running along the window wall.

OPPOSITE Franck and Laurent have a great regard for the craft of taxidermy, believing that it allows the beauty of animals to be appreciated after their death. The two stuffed birds on this table have been teamed with an unusual table lamp, itself shaped to resemble a bird.

ABOVE RIGHT Thanks to Franck's ingenuity, a 19th-century daybed has been given a new personality by the addition of an iron frame topped by a gilded crown.
RIGHT During many years of exposure to the elements, this classical statue has acquired a patina of age.

Legend has it that this upside-down tart was created in the 1880s at a hotel run by the Tatin sisters in the Sologne region, south of Paris. While making traditional apple pie, Stéphanie Tatin was distracted from her task and allowed the fruit to cook in butter and sugar for too long. In an attempt to rescue the dish, she put the pastry on top of the apple for cooking. When it came out of the oven, the tart was inverted onto a serving plate – and it proved an instant hit. A tarte tatin pan or other round flameproof baking dish is required for this recipe. Crème fraîche is the best accompaniment.

Tarte tatin

1.5 kg/3½ lbs. apples
  such as Cox's, Braeburn
  or Granny Smith
150 g/1 stick plus
  2 tablespoons
  unsalted butter
150 g/¾ cup (caster) sugar

sweet pastry/pâte brisée
200 g/1½ cups plain/
  all-purpose flour
2 teaspoons (caster) sugar
100 g/7 tablespoons cold
  unsalted butter, cut into
  pieces
a pinch of salt

Serves 8

To make the pastry, put the flour, sugar, butter and salt in a food processor and, using the pulse button, process until the butter is broken down (about 5–10 pulses).

Add 3 tablespoons cold water and pulse just until the dough forms coarse crumbs; add 1 more tablespoon water if necessary, but do not do more than 10 pulses.

Transfer the pastry to a sheet of baking parchment, form into a ball and flatten to a disc. Wrap up in the paper and let stand for 30–60 minutes.

Roll out the pastry to a disc the diameter of the pan; turn the pan upside down on the rolled-out pastry, press down and trace around the edge with the tip of a sharp knife. Transfer the pastry round to a baking sheet and chill until needed.

Peel, core and quarter the apples. Set aside.

Put the butter and sugar in the baking pan and melt over high heat, stirring to blend. Remove from the heat and arrange the apples in the pan in 2 circles. The inner circle should go in the opposite direction to the outer one.

Return to the heat and cook for 30 minutes. From this point, watch the apples carefully and cook for a further 5–15 minutes, until the liquid thickens and turns a golden caramel colour. Remove from the heat and put the disc of pastry on top, gently tucking in the edges.

Preheat the oven to 200°C (400°F) Gas 6. Transfer the tart to the preheated oven and bake for 45–60 minutes, until browned. Remove from the oven and let cool slightly. Invert onto a serving plate while still warm (or the caramel will harden, making it too difficult). Serve hot, warm or at room temperature.

Daily bread

Bread in all its myriad styles, shapes and sizes is an integral part of French life, and nothing is more redolent of France than the sight of a beret-wearing workman cycling home for lunch with his pannier full of freshly baked baguettes.

Althoughly closely associated with France, the baguette is now made all over the world, and different methods of baking have been introduced to speed up production. To preserve the integrity of the original, and to secure the future of the *boulangerie*, in 1993 a law was passed in France that the *baguette de tradition* and other artisanal breads could be made only with flour, water, salt and yeast. (Most French bread is made with a flour called Type 55.)

Bakeries across France are now restoring the art of making bread in wood-fired ovens constructed of brick and stone, in which the loaves are moved around with a long-handled wooden shovel called a peel. *Pain de campagne* – a crusty, chewy, well-flavoured loaf made from a flour that retains a small proportion of bran, giving an off-white colour – is among the breads that benefits from this method.

One of the champions of traditional breadmaking was Lionel Poilâne (1945–2002), who baked loaves called *miches* in one of the last remaining wood-fired ovens in Paris. Young bakers have followed Poilâne's lead, using organic and stone-ground flours, and *levain* (sourdough); others have reduced their use of yeast and returned to the long fermentation necessary for a superior baguette.

Nothing is more redolent of France than the sight of a beret-wearing workman cycling home or lunch with his pannier full of freshly baked baguettes.

Post-industrial living space

Virginie Denny and Alfonso Vallès have created a perfect home for themselves on the edge of Paris, in the unlikely setting of an old button factory. Built in the 1920s in Bagnolet, an eastern suburb of the city, the former industrial building was stripped out in 2005 and divided into 13 residential units. When the couple took possession of theirs, it was no more than an empty shell, but they set about transforming it into a comfortable apartment-cum-art-gallery.

THIS PICTURE In dramatic contrast to the pair of miniatures resting quietly on the back of the sofa, one of Alfonso's startling portraits dominates the contemporary living space. The modern elements of the room are neutralized by the soft furnishings, while natural light gives a surface sheen to the polished-concrete floor.
OPPOSITE BELOW An ever-changing display of cards, sketches and photographs suspended from string and clothes pegs adorns the office wall.

OPPOSITE Large sliding doors allow natural light to stream into the eating and cooking area, while the verdant patio suggests a much more rural setting than suburban Paris.
LEFT AND BELOW Alfonso and Virginie opted for an ultra-modern fitted kitchen in concrete and brushed steel. Vintage wooden chairs and recycled wooden doors introduce a softer feel into what might otherwise have been a rather stark and chilly environment.
RIGHT The juxtaposition of paintbrushes with flowers in vases draws attention to the similarities between the two very different types of object.

'We did everything ourselves except for the plumbing,' says Virginie, a stylist. 'We laid the floor, put in the electrical wiring and designed the layout of the rooms – all without an architect.' The original floor was lowered and an upper level and staircase were installed, increasing the size of the living space. Windows at the front and back extend all the way up to the roof, flooding the space with natural light.

To retain the industrial spirit of the former factory, they used materials such as concrete and metal but included recycled wood and muted colours to soften the effect. Decorative objects and furniture were bought from flea markets, including the ornate metal stair rail and the collection of lamps. 'Each piece of furniture has a history,' says Virginie. 'And we like to mix styles.'

The master bedroom is in the centre of the house on the ground floor. It has no exterior windows, so the couple inserted an internal window into one wall, allowing light to stream in from the living area. At night, curtains are pulled across for privacy. The bedroom's most unusual feature is a large bathtub set in concrete. 'Many of our friends regard it as impractical,' says Virginie, 'but I enjoy having a bath in the bedroom.'

ABOVE The smaller bedroom has been configured to suit the couple's young son Leon. The bed is raised higher than normal, and drawers have been incorporated underneath for storing toys. In contrast with the other rooms in the house, the floor is wooden rather than concrete, providing a warmer surface for Leon to play on. His bedside light takes the form of a white dove.

RIGHT AND ABOVE RIGHT Perhaps the most extraordinary aspect of this apartment is the combined bathroom and bedroom. Above the bedside table, made of old wooden filing drawers, is another painting by Alfonso.

THIS PAGE On one side of his studio, Alfonso has a created a simple office, consisting of ittle more than a trestle table, a wooden chair and the inevitable cluster of paintbrushes. The lines of poetry on the wall were twisted into shape by Alfonso using lengths of thin metal wire.

The bedside table, a stack of old drawer units, is used to display cherished flea-market finds.

Decorating the walls is the responsibility of Alfonso, a painter, who has his own studio in the apartment. His dramatic figurative paintings are shown off to good effect against the unobtrusive background colours. 'I don't paint anything specially for the house,' he says. 'Virginie just comes into my studio, takes a piece of work and hangs it where she thinks it will look good.'

Stairs lead up from the studio to the mezzanine, where there is a guest room and a balcony on each side. Virginie and Alfonso use the balconies as home offices and, thanks to the tall windows at each end of the apartment, the spaces are filled with natural light. Another appealing feature is the patio garden. 'It's very quiet here and there are few buildings overlooking us,' says Virginie.

Old and new, wood and metal, concrete and glass have been combined to create a family home with huge warmth and positive energy in this contemporary post-industrial space.

ABOVE, LEFT TO RIGHT Outside Leon's bedroom is a birdcage with stuffed birds, and fixed to the wall above it is a row of wooden printer's blocks spelling out his name. As elsewhere, paintbrushes are treated as works of art in their own right.

BELOW, LEFT TO RIGHT All sorts of surprising items can be found throughout the apartment. Some have a practical purpose, while others, such as old paperbacks and weaver's bobbins, have been chosen for their texture, tactility or decorative effect.

THIS PAGE Overflowing with canvases and artist's equipment, Alfonso's studio benefits from an abundance of northern light. His paintings are propped up against the wall and set on easels, while brushes of all shapes and sizes are kept in various containers and glass pots. The industrial-style drawer unit has been fitted with wheels so that it is easy to move around.

L'Esprit de la Mer

2

de la Mer

Brittany and Normandy

RIGHT The antique armchairs in the living room are called *chaises à la reine* and date from the reign of Louis XV (1715–74). Behind them is a magnificent *buffet à deux corps* (one cupboard above another), whose subtle colouring harmonizes with the upholstery.

LEFT AND BELOW Much of the painted woodwork gives the impression of venerable age. Some pieces are genuinely old, but others, such as the kitchen doors, have been distressed to make them seem older than they are.

OPPOSITE Secluded corners designed for relaxing are a feature of the garden. Here, the decorative approach is simplicity itself: a small circular metal table, geraniums in a Versailles planter and wire birdcages adorning the walls.

Splendid solitude

Annie-Camille Kuentzmann puts a high value on tranquillity and solitude, and for that reason she loves living alone in this wonderful old barn in a hamlet south of the Seine valley. She moved here from a much smaller house in the middle of a village, where she felt that there was no room to breathe – nor was there nearly enough room for Annie-Camille's astonishing collection of 18th-century French furniture, which includes 26 *fauteuils* (armchairs).

The hamlet is located at the meeting place of three of France's 27 regions: Normandy, Ile de France and Centre. The nearest town is Ivry-la-Bataille, named after a battle of 1590, which stands on the river Eure, a tributary of the Seine. And, just 15 km (9 miles) north of here, the Seine itself follows its extraordinarily serpentine course to the sea at Le Havre. Another local landmark is the original Boursin cheese factory at Croisy-sur-Eure.

When Annie-Camille took possession of the property in 2001, there was no need for exterior alteration. The hamlet had suffered severe damage during the Second World War – taking a hit from a stray bomb dropped by an American plane returning from an anti-German raid – but previous owners had restored the barn to its former glory. However, she did do some structural work inside, putting up a wall between the kitchen and the vast living room. Along one wall of the living room are four pairs of elegant French windows opening onto the garden.

The traditional, steeply pitched barn roof was still in place, and its huge height allowed for the construction of a mezzanine floor, which now includes guest accommodation. Annie-Camille also made a large bedroom for herself and a bathroom with an antique bathtub and sink.

'I have a passion for old things,' says Annie-Camille, 'especially French things from the 18th century.' She describes herself as a student of art history, archaeology and ethnology, and her wide-ranging interests are reflected in the choice of beautiful objects displayed in her home.

One of the most striking features of the house is the multitude of portraits in pastels and oils. In fact, there are now more than 100 of these, all dating from the 18th century, and most picked up at *brocantes*. Eyes – albeit friendly eyes – watching you in every room create the impression that the house is much more populated than it actually is. '*C'est une folie!*' says Annie-Camille, while ruefully admitting that there is no space for any more of her beloved portraits.

All the floors are covered in traditional terracotta tiles from Normandy, and all the walls have been painted white, to show off the works of art to best effect. The pitched

THIS PAGE AND OPPOSITE One of Annie-Camille's few structural changes was to erect a wall between the living room and kitchen, which doubles as a cosy eating area. The terracotta floor tiles, laid in a traditional diamond design, are from the Pays de Bray in Normandy. A mixture of salvaged tiles, plain and patterned, has been used to cover walls and surfaces. The slim rectangular white tiles behind the sink recall those found on the walls of the Paris Métro.

ceiling in the full-height living room has been left in its original state, while the ceilings in the other rooms consist of white-painted wooden beams and planks.

The idyll is completed by a well-tended garden that is overflowing with plants, flowers and trees. Among the agricultural outbuildings that Annie-Camille acquired with the barn is a shed that she has converted into a little summerhouse – a place to linger on sunny days, a place that embodies its owner's dream of tranquil living in the countryside.

ABOVE RIGHT The height of the roof made it possible to install a mezzanine floor in the old barn, which Annie-Camille has used to create an intimate guest bedroom. The brilliant red colour in the patterned bedspread is rose madder, one of the dyes used in the printing of traditional toiles.
RIGHT AND ABOVE A vintage claw-foot bathtub occupies pride of place in the bathroom, while a pretty gathered curtain conceals storage space beneath the antique basin. The gilded bed canopy over the bath dates from the reign of Louis XIV (1643–1715).

THIS PAGE On this Louis XV daybed in a corner of the living room are two quilts – one antique, the other new – as well as cushions in different fabrics, including one made in an 18th-century *toile de Beautiran*.

A harvest from the sea

Exploring local food markets is one of the most rewarding ways to get to know France. In Brittany, most towns have their own weekly market, usually on the same day all year round. There you can enjoy the sights and sounds and take in the smells of Breton oysters, mussels, cheeses, crêpes, cider, honey and locally grown fruit, herbs and vegetables, not to mention barbecued local sausages, fish stews and free-range chickens cooked on a *rôtisserie*.

If you get up early enough, you can attend the auctions of fresh fish.

The sea is the life-blood of Brittany, which has a jagged coastline stretching for more than 1,700 km (1,050 miles) and numerous small harbours populated by fleets of trawlers with richly painted hulls. Fishing is the region's most important economic activity, ahead of tourism and agriculture. Much of the fresh fish and seafood is exported to other parts of France or abroad, but enough is retained in Brittany to satisfy local demand from residents and visitors. If you get up early enough, you can attend the auctions of fresh fish at places such as Audierne, Concarneau and Lorient, where the catch is usually on sale within 30 minutes of the fleet's arrival in port.

Normandy also has a long coastline, and is the chief oyster-cultivating, as well as biggest scallop-exporting, region in France. Shrimp, lobster, herring, trout, turbot and sole are found in abundance in markets and at restaurants. After oysters, the most popular dishes on the menu are *coquilles Saint-Jacques*, *moules marinières* and multi-tiered platters of *fruits de mer*.

Steaming mussels open in a big pot with wine and flavourings to create the traditional *moules marinières* takes only about 5 minutes, but preparation can be fiddly and time-consuming. One option is to buy mussels that have already been cleaned and de-bearded, and the wine stock can be prepared in advance. You will need a large piece of muslin/cheesecloth to strain the cooking liquid. When the dish is ready, take the pot to the table and ladle out the mussels first, then serve the delicious soupy juices to be mopped up with hot crusty bread.

Moules marinières

3 kg/6½ lbs. fresh mussels
4 tablespoons olive oil
3 garlic cloves, very finely chopped
3 onions, very finely chopped
200 ml/¾ cup dry white wine
a good pinch of dried red pepper flakes
4 tablespoons coarsely chopped fresh flat-leaf parsley
lemon wedges

Serves 6

Scrub the mussels well under cold running water, knock off any barnacles and pull off the beards. Discard any broken mussels and any that won't close when they are tapped on the work surface. Drain in a colander.

Heat the oil in a large, deep saucepan. Add the garlic and onions and fry for 10 minutes, until softened but not coloured. Add the wine, pepper flakes and 200 ml/¾ cup water, bring to the boil and simmer for 10 minutes.

Add the mussels, cover and cook over high heat for about 5 minutes, shaking the pan every now and then, until the mussels have opened. Discard any that remain closed.

Strain the mussels through a muslin/cheesecloth-lined colander set over a bowl or saucepan. Keep the mussels warm in the colander and boil the mussel liquid to reduce slightly. Stir in the chopped parsley. Pile the mussels into warmed bowls, and pour over the hot broth. Serve with lemon wedges.

A feast of blues

On the north-east coast of Brittany, close to its border with Normandy, stands the walled city of St Malo, once notorious for its corsairs, or pirates, but now better known as a busy ferry port, with services to England and the Channel Islands. Outside the city, high on a rocky promontory, is this imposing creeper-clad house – the holiday retreat of the Sabouret family from Paris. Laurence and Yves Sabouret and their three children escape there as often as they can.

ABOVE LEFT The steeply sloping slate roof and tall chimneys are typical of an architectural style associated with this part of the Breton coast. A profusion of native plants rambles over the surrounding rocks.
ABOVE RIGHT Framed by dark-needled pines, the views from the terrace are breathtaking.

RIGHT A shaded terrace high above the sea is the perfect place for an alfresco summer lunch. Its white-painted floor and railings are redolent of the tropics. The various blues in the china, glass and cutlery/flatware echo the house's colour scheme, while a red-and-white-striped tablecloth adds zest to the occasion.

OPPOSITE In response to the strong character of the house itself, the interior scheme has deliberately been kept simple, but it still makes a powerful impact. Colours are confined to soft neutral shades enlivened with bright sea blues, navy and other primary colours. The sofas in the living room, covered in creamy white cotton with dark blue piping, make a refreshing complement to the blue curtains.
LEFT AND FAR LEFT These teak sunbeds with their comfortably raked backs and footrests are ideal for an afternoon snooze. The lifebelts are decorative rather than functional.

Built about a century ago, the building has a steeply pitched roof of steely-grey slates pierced by large red chimneys. It conforms to a style of architecture found all along this coast – 'inherited from the Normandy example seen at Deauville but with a typically Breton twist', in the words of Laurence Sabouret. In the main living room, the walls are covered with traditional oak *boiseries* and there is a large fireplace, also in oak, carved with Breton motifs.

Most of the windows in the house have sturdy louvred shutters, giving protection against the hot sun in summer and the fierce winds of winter. The view from the terrace is breathtaking: framed by the branches of pines and the rocky outcrops is the sea, dotted in summer with scores of yachts.

The northern light along these coasts is more subtle than the bright light of the Mediterranean and over the years has attracted a host of artists, including Monet, Boudin, Signac, Picasso and many lesser-known names.

Considerable artistic talent is also evident inside this house, where the decoration throughout has been inspired by its seaside location. Rather than paint over the dark oak

panelling and destroy some of the building's character, Laurence has used an abundance of white to lighten the interior, along with many different shades of blue. She favours blues that evoke the Caribbean, the French Riviera and the Greek islands, as well as Brittany itself. When the weather is good in Brittany, she says, 'The sea can be like a light-green or blue lagoon. The water is transparent.'

To enhance the illusion of being in the tropics, the railings of the terrace and its floor are all painted bright white, while the décor is nautical. There are plenty of teak-framed deck loungers with off-white cotton cushions, and there is an awning to provide shade from the sun on hot days.

Indoors from the terrace is the main living area, where luxuriously comfortable sofas have soft white covers crisply piped in blue and arranged around a patterned rug in the same tones. On the white covers is a mixture of cushions, some covered in plain blue, others in a geometrical pattern and yet others in an Indienne design. (Indiennes were inspired by textile imports from the East in the mid-17th century and remain as popular today as toiles de Jouy.)

RIGHT AND OPPOSITE Dark oak panelling, beams and ornate arched doors are prominent features on the ground floor. To retain the original integrity of the interior, it was decided not to paint the panels and doors in a lighter colour. Instead, the décor has been updated by the display of objects with maritime associations, including maps and models of boats.

LEFT, BELOW AND INSET The Sabourets are generous hosts, and the constant stream of visitors creates plenty of opportunities for the beautiful blue-and-white pottery and napkins to be put to good use. In accordance with the main colour scheme, even the knives and forks have blue handles.

THIS PAGE A palette of brilliant sea blues and turquoises offset by shades of white and cream unifies the decorative objects on display with the more practical elements such as rugs, tables and curtains. Groups of shells, sea-washed pebbles and transparent blue glass bottles and lamps act as constant reminders of the proximity of the ocean. When the weather is warm, the French doors are left open to admit cooling sea breezes.

To these elements have been added white Roman blinds and a white cabriole-legged French table, covered with sea-washed shells and a collection of cerulean-blue glass, models and paintings of yachts.

The same colours are repeated in the main bedroom – white curtains, a blue patterned wallpaper and blue-and-white bed linen, while elsewhere Provençal tablecloths and blue-and-white European and Chinese ceramics are teamed with navigational charts and more nautical pictures.

When the Sabourets have friends to stay, the days are structured around carefully planned meals, while guests have freedom in between to do just as they please. In typically French fashion, food is a major preoccupation, and the mornings often start with Laurence and Yves making a shopping list. 'I bend from the balcony like a diva in a theatre,' laughs Laurence, 'with the terrace and the long sandy beach and the musical sound of the water on the rocks – and we argue about the menu.'

By ten o'clock, if the weather is fine, the cushions are laid out on the wooden chairs, and beach towels and the parasols are in position for a day of lazy sunbathing, interspersed with swimming, sailing or a spot of golf. At 7.30pm, the party gathers on the terrace to admire the view. 'The light is wonderful, pure, gentle for the eyes. The rocks are burning in red and rose, and the air is suspended,' says Laurence.

ABOVE RIGHT One of the few rooms in the house in which pattern has been given a leading role is the main bedroom, which has a flamboyant geometrical wallpaper. Yet even here the basic blues, creams and white are in control – and the shirt hanging in front of the window is just the right shade of blue. The floor has been painted white to enhance the strong light from the sea.
INSET RIGHT The collection of shells arranged in neat rows includes examples of limpet, mussel, scallop and cockle shells – all of which can be found in abundance on nearby beaches.

Cheeses of Normandy

Cattle grazing the lush pastures of Normandy produce milk that is naturally rich in protein and fat, giving the local cheeses their soft, creamy texture. Normandy's most famous cheese is Camembert, which became entrenched in French popular cuisine after it was issued to French troops during the First World War. Also highly prized are Pont-l'Evêque and Livarot.

Camembert was reputedly invented during the French Revolution by a Normandy farmer, Marie Harel, under the guidance of Charles-Jean Bonvoust, an abbot from Brie who was fleeing from persecution. The farmer had given refuge to the priest, and in exchange he passed on some wise advice about maturing cheeses.

The AOC (*Appellation d'Origine Contrôlée*) variety Camembert de Normandie must by law be made from unpasteurized milk, which gives it a rich and complex flavour. When ripe, it has a runny interior similar to the milder Brie. Unlike Brie, which is made in large, flat wheels, Camembert is made in individual cheeses 11 cm (4¼ inches) in diameter. More than 50 million AOC Camembert de Normandie rounds are sold each year.

Pont-l'Evêque has a springy consistency and a 'washed rind'. This means the cheese has been washed or rubbed in brine, wine or cider, giving it a rich fruity flavour and the rind a deep orange shade. Livarot is known as the 'Colonel' because of its appearance: it has five strips of sedge grass wrapped around its sides. Made by the same process as Pont l'Evêque, it has a typical washed rind and a pungent aroma.

The AOC variety Camembert de Normandie must by law be made from unpasteurized milk, which gives it a rich and complex flavour.

You can't go far in Brittany without coming across a *crêperie*. Here you will find not only a wide choice of sweet pancakes but also the distinctive *galettes bretonnes*, large thin pancakes made from buckwheat flour that are folded over to envelop savoury fillings ranging from ham and egg to *escargots* (snails). This recipe is for the classic sweet pancake, often served with a little butter and a sprinkling of sugar. To achieve a light, crisp result, leave the batter to stand for at least 1 hour before cooking. Finishing touches include a melting knob/pat of butter or a generous glug of calvados or Grand Marnier.

Crêpes

250 g/scant 2 cups plain/
  all-purpose flour
3 large/US extra-large
  eggs, beaten
500 ml/2 cups whole milk
2 tablespoons sugar, plus
  extra to serve
unsalted butter, for cooking
  and to serve
lemon halves, to serve

Serves 4–6

Put the flour in a large bowl and make a hollow in the middle. Pour the eggs into the hollow. Using a wooden spoon, gradually beat the eggs into the flour. Stir well to get rid of any lumps. Pour the milk in slowly, stirring constantly, until completely blended. Stir in the sugar. Let stand for at least 1 hour.

Heat a small, non-stick frying pan over medium heat. Add a knob/pat of butter, melt and swirl to coat. Add a ladle of batter to the pan and swirl to spread thinly but evenly. Cook until the crêpe is browning around the edges and bubbly in the middle, then flip over and cook for a few minutes longer.

As a rule, the first few crêpes are not perfect because it takes a while for the pan to get to just the right temperature. Continue cooking until all the batter is used up, occasionally adding more butter as needed. Serve with a sprinkling of sugar and a knob/pat of butter.

La, tout n'est
qu'ordre
et beauté,
Luxe, calme et
volupté.

(There, all is order and beauty,
Luxury, peace, and pleasure.)

Les Fleurs du Mal, *Charles Baudelaire*

(There, all is order and beauty,)
Luxury, peace, and pleasure.)

Les Fleurs du Mal, Charles Baudelaire

BELOW Outdoor living is celebrated to the full in the grounds of this Normandy farmhouse. The large and abundant garden includes several shady spots where a table and chairs can be set up for an impromptu midday meal.

ABOVE An open-sided barn is used for storing ladders and garden equipment, as well as items associated with enjoying life in the open air.
BELOW Reflecting Julie's fondness for using wire artefacts as decorative objects, a set of three wire hanging baskets provides useful additional storage in the barn.
OPPOSITE Not far from the lake is an old agricultural building that is used for informal dining in summer.

A subtle harmony

Julie Prisca is an acclaimed designer of modern furniture and lighting. She has her own shop in the rue de Verneuil, in the St-Germain-des-Prés area of Paris, and has recently launched an online store. Whenever she needs some respite from city life, Julie escapes to this beautiful old farmhouse in Normandy, which is furnished with many of her own creations, including sofas, daybeds, lamps, chairs and tables.

ABOVE Since the house is built around a courtyard, many of the rooms receive light through windows on both sides. Among these is the chic living room, which has an attractive painted commode, or bow-fronted chest of drawers, set against one wall. Sisal matting has been used to cover the floor.

Julie's house consists of a converted brick barn dating from the mid-19th century, with a ground area of 320 square metres (3,400 square feet).

This imposing building – large enough to accommodate five bedrooms and four bathrooms – is surrounded by a park of 1.7 hectares (4.2 acres), including a river and a small lake. In summer, Julie and her family and friends spend much of their time lazing beside the lake, where a rustic chalet serves as an informal dining room. This is a place where outdoor living is enjoyed to the full.

When Julie and her husband came here in 2006, the barn consisted of no more than four walls and a roof, so, as well as repairing

the basic structure, they had to design and build the interior from scratch. They put in a large number of glass doors and windows, including portholes, so that light would permeate the whole house. Now, when the sun shines, the light is so strong that it conveys the impression of being under water.

Modern elements of the decoration include a polished concrete floor and metal door and window frames that were specially made in the designer's workshops and finished in black gloss paint. Julie Prisca's approach is to create simple, unfussy backdrops against which to display a mixture of modern and antique – preferably 18th-century – objects and pictures. She favours a restrained colour palette of plum, chocolate, various greys, taupe and pale green. 'I hate ostentation,' she says. The clean

TOP The curvaceous, fine-lined daybed is made of wrought iron, a common material in French country homes.
ABOVE This porthole window with intricate glazing bars was installed by Julie.
RIGHT Many of the traditional pieces of furniture in the house, including the huge cupboard at the back of the living room, were discovered at local *brocantes*. Minimalist curtains make the most of the natural light.

lines of the modern furniture give it a timeless elegance, allowing Julie to achieve a subtle harmony between old and new. One of Julie's design heroes is Jean–Michel Frank – champion of spare, understated luxury – who in the 1930s lived and worked in the very same Paris street as that in which Julie has her shop.

The main living room of the farmhouse covers 50 square metres (540 square feet), with walls painted in biscuit and taupe colours and a wonderfully open feel. Most of the decorative objects on display either come originally from Africa or Asia or were picked up at local *brocantes*. Double doors open onto the dining area, which is separated from the kitchen by shelves of wire netting displaying a collection of old glasses, carafes and silver plate. The walls are the colour of dark chocolate on the dining-room side and very pale pink on the kitchen side.

The kitchen is sleek and modern in style, but Julie was against the idea of installing closed cupboards. Instead, she has arranged plates, glassware and cooking utensils on open shelves so that they are both on display and easy to reach. There is a central island with a built-in oven and hob/stove. The work surfaces are in very dark wood or stainless steel. As with other elements of the house, everything has been made to measure in Julie's workshops.

TOP Eye-catching containers for storage and display, such as this wire basket on top of a glass-sided cabinet, can be seen throughout the house. **ABOVE** Adorned with items from Julie's shop in Paris, the bathroom reflects a new interpretation of a traditional style. Occupying the middle of the room is a basin set into a freestanding unit supported by a wrought-iron base. The tub is sited beneath the window to take advantage of the natural light. **RIGHT** These mismatched plates are treasured possessions, collected over the years.

THIS PAGE The subtle use of colour, with grey blues fading into greeny blues, is evident in this bedroom entrance area. Julie Prisca's signature colours, which she combines with great artistry, are pale green, prune, mauve and a range of greys and whites.

Apples, cider and calvados

The abundant apple orchards of Normandy and Brittany have been renowned for centuries as the source of three popular French drinks: cider, calvados (apple brandy) and pommeau (a mixture of two-thirds apple juice and one-third calvados).

A good cider depends on the right combination of sweet, sour and bittersweet apples – some ciders include as many as two dozen varieties. After harvesting and dry storage, the pulp is slowly pressed, and the liquid is allowed to ferment naturally in airtight vats. It can then be filtered and pasteurized. French cider is fermented in such a way that some of the natural sugar is preserved and it is bottled before fermentation has finished. This gives a sweet, sparkling, low-alcohol but richly tannic-flavoured drink. In Brittany, cider is usually served in a traditional ceramic bowl or cup called a *bolée* rather than a glass.

In Brittany, cider is usually served in a traditional ceramic bowl or cup called a bolée rather than a glass.

Over 200 varieties of apple are specially
grown for distillation into calvados. Several
varieties may be used in one brand, ranging
from very sweet to very tart. The fruit is
harvested from mid-October to December and
is then pressed into a juice that is fermented
into a dry cider. It is subsequently distilled into
an *eau-de-vie*, which is blended and matured
for a minimum of two years in casks to produce
a rich amber nectar. The longer the maturation,
the mellower the final product.

Le trou Normand, or 'the Norman hole', is
a tot of calvados taken between courses during
a long meal in order to revive the appetite.

Leg of pork simmered for several hours in cider is wonderfully tender, and the luxuriously rich sauce produced by this cooking method intensifies the subtle flavour of the meat. *Pommes de terre* (potatoes) are added for the last hour of cooking, and the roast is served with the traditional accompaniment of lightly stewed *pommes* (apples), along with the cooking sauce and a little cream. Apples and cream are both inextricably associated with Normandy cuisine.

Porc au cidre aux deux pommes

30 g/2 tablespoons unsalted butter

2 onions, sliced

1 tablespoon sunflower/safflower oil

1 pork middle leg roast, about 1.75 kg/3¾ lbs., fat trimmed

1.5 litres/6 cups (hard) dry cider

2 sprigs of thyme

800 g/1¾ lbs. new potatoes, peeled and halved lengthways

125 ml/½ cup double/heavy cream

coarse sea salt and freshly ground black pepper

apples
60 g/4 tablespoons unsalted butter

5 tart apples, such as Braeburn or Cox's, peeled, cored and sliced

Serves 4

Preheat the oven to 150°C (300°F) Gas 2.

Melt the butter in a large flameproof casserole dish. Add the onions and cook gently for about 5 minutes, until softened but not browned. Remove the onions. Add the oil, then increase the heat, add the pork and cook until browned all over. Remove and season well with salt and pepper.

Add some of the cider to the casserole dish, heat and scrape the bottom of the pan.

Return the meat and onions to the casserole dish and add the remaining cider and thyme. Season lightly and bring to the boil. Boil for 1 minute, skim off any foam that rises to the surface, then reduce the heat, cover and cook in the preheated oven for 4 hours. Turn the pork regularly and taste and adjust the seasoning halfway through the cooking time.

One hour before the end of the cooking time, add the potatoes and continue cooking. Remove from the oven, transfer the pork and potatoes to a plate and cover with foil to keep them warm. Cook the sauce over high heat for 10–15 minutes to reduce slightly. Taste and adjust the seasoning.

Meanwhile, to cook the apples, melt the butter in a large frying pan, add the apples and cook over high heat for 5–10 minutes, until browned and tender. Do not crowd the pan; use 2 pans if necessary.

To serve, slice the pork and arrange on plates with the potatoes and apples. Stir the cream into the sauce and serve immediately.

La Douceur de Vivre

de Vivre

3

Poitou-Charentes and Aquitaine

Colour palettes

Natural light affects the way colours are perceived, and in France the quality and intensity of light changes dramatically from north to south, and from west to east. These natural differences are reflected in the way colours are used decoratively. The further north you are, the greater the predominance of paler and more limpid shades, echoing the huge northern skies. In the predominantly sunny south, the tones are stronger and more definite.

French whites are sometimes creamy, sometimes touched with grey, and often have the soft, granular texture of white chalk. It is not unusual for several different shades of white to be used together. Grey is ubiquitous; a pale version of grey was the popular colour of the 17th and early 18th centuries, often contrasted with off-white. This domestic grey is luminous, perhaps with a pale pink or blue base that gives it a warm or fresh tone.

Grey diversifies into blue, and most French blues are reflective colours, used to calm and soothe. From grey also come mauve and lilac – either as vivid as the iris or closer to the quiet, almost misty tones that are quintessentially French. Pinks and peaches appear almost organic, seeming as though they have emerged from the colour of the original plaster rather than having been applied on top of it.

Like the Scandinavians, the French are fond of painted furniture, and the soft and subtle colours they tend to favour – reminiscent of the patina of old wood – are every bit as effective on furniture as they are on walls. Distressed effects are often thought to give a more authentic feel than flat colour, especially in country homes.

France has the only two things toward which we drift as we grow older – intelligence and good manners.

F. Scott Fitzgerald

France has the only two things
toward which we drift as we grow
older – intelligence and good manners.

F Scott Fitzgerald

This chicken dish from the Basque region of south-west France has many variations. Some recipes use only green (bell) peppers, others use only onions and chillies. The most authentic version includes *piment d'Espelette*, a delicious little chilli grown in the Basque country and widely used in local dishes. *Poulet basquaise* should be pleasantly spicy without being overpowering – so, whichever chilli you choose, resist the temptation to overdo it. Serve with rice.

Poulet Basquaise

2 tablespoons olive oil
1 free-range chicken, about 2 kg/4½ lbs., cut into 8 pieces
2 onions, sliced
2 red (bell) peppers, halved, seeded and sliced
2 yellow (bell) peppers, halved, seeded and sliced
2–4 large garlic cloves, crushed
2 small hot green chillies, seeded and thinly sliced (or ½ teaspoon dried chilli flakes)

1 thick slice jambon de Bayonne or other unsmoked ham, about 2 cm/¾ inch thick and 160 g/6 oz., cut into strips
1 kg/2 ¼ lbs. ripe tomatoes, skinned, seeded and chopped
coarse sea salt and freshly ground black pepper

Serves 4

Heat the oil in a large frying pan with a lid, add the chicken pieces skin-side down and cook for 5–10 minutes, until brown. Don't crowd the pan; if you can't fit all the pieces at once, brown in batches. Transfer the chicken to a plate, season well with salt and set aside.

Add the onions and (bell) peppers to the pan, season with salt and black pepper, then cook over medium heat for 15–20 minutes, until soft. Stir in the garlic, chillies and ham and cook for 1 minute. Add the tomatoes, mix well, then add all the chicken pieces and bury them under the sauce.

Cover and cook over low heat for 30–40 minutes, until the chicken is tender.

OPPOSITE In one corner of the living room is a vintage *chaise longue* covered in a hessian throw. Perfectly positioned to give good views of the garden, it offers the ideal spot for an afternoon snooze.

BELOW AND BELOW RIGHT The study area overlooks the large central courtyard of the house. From the oak floor to the makeshift low table, reclaimed wood is the dominant material in this room.

RIGHT The bookshelves on the dining-room wall began life as a baker's display unit. Terracotta pots on the top shelf were once used to store cooking fats.

An island paradise

In 1988, life changed for ever in Ile de Ré, off the west coast of central France, with the opening of a 3-km (2-mile) toll-bridge linking the island with the city of La Rochelle on the mainland. No longer did residents and visitors have to rely on an inefficient and overstretched ferry service. In addition, for those travelling by TGV, France's high-speed train, La Rochelle is now a mere three-hour journey from Paris. Since the arrival of the bridge and the train service, the island has become ever more popular as a sophisticated tourist destination.

LEFT AND BELOW Old stone walls are left exposed in the kitchen. The rough cupboard doors under the sink make an interesting contrast with the sleek steel appliances on either side. The shelf above is lined with 18th-century truffle jars, while hanging from it is a sturdy wooden coathanger supporting glass candle-holders.

OPPOSITE In the centre of the kitchen is a 1950s table with a stripped top, flanked by army-surplus folding chairs. The dark grey slates on the floor were salvaged from Serge's family home in Brittany. Above the fireplace, the portrait of a customs officer – one of Françoise's family heirlooms – adds a nautical touch.

Just 30 km (20 miles) long and 5 km (3 miles) wide, Ile de Ré is a haven of tranquillity with an exceptionally sunny microclimate. The sailing resort of Ars-en-Ré, on the island's north-west coast, where Françoise and Serge Madec established their homewares shop more than 20 years ago, has been described as one of France's most beautiful villages. The shop in question is Côté Jardin, an emporium of beautiful antiques and second-hand pieces for both house and garden. The theme that links all the disparate items in Côté Jardin is the idea of *racines*, or roots – meaning that everything must have an interesting provenance.

It is this same theme that characterizes the various homes that Françoise and Serge have created for themselves on the island. The couple share a passion for acquiring neglected old houses and renovating them. Their current home is the third property they have restored in Ars-en-Ré. It is barely 100 metres (330 feet) from Côté Jardin and a similar distance from the village church. Just like the contents of the shop, all the pieces in the house have a story to tell.

When the couple bought this property in 2002, it had been uninhabited for several years and there was plenty of work to be done. Dating from the mid-19th century, the

RIGHT AND FAR RIGHT Even the spaces between rooms are carefully thought out. The landing on the first floor, which gives access to the bedrooms, is graced with a marble-topped pedestal table that once did service in a bistro..The table is now used for a still-life display incorporating various glass objects, a charming old mirror and an industrial-sized bobbin encircled with thick yarn.

original dwelling was simplicity itself, based on a barn-like building containing an olive press and two adjoining rooms arranged around a U-shaped courtyard of 45 square metres (480 square feet). According to Françoise, this style of house is typical of those inhabited by the peasant farming communities that until quite recently dominated the island. Many of the farmers made a modest living from cultivating potatoes and a few vines.

The basic configuration of the house had remained unchanged over the years. What appealed most to the Madecs was the high-ceilinged central space, covering more than 70 square metres (750 square feet), which had been used as a garage. Inspired by the obvious potential of the building, the couple embarked on a process of conversion and renovation that took six months.

LEFT A pair of delicate 19th-century side chairs, one positioned either side of the headboard, have found a new role as bedside tables in the master bedroom. The headboard itself was recycled from a length of old wall panelling. These and similar objects that can be found at Côté Jardin, the Madecs' shop in the village, are on show throughout the house.

OPPOSITE As in other rooms, most of the elements of the bathroom have a story to tell. The chequerboard floor is made up of old cement tiles that were rescued from a salvage yard and restored. The magnificent claw-foot bathtub came from Françoise's family home, and the elaborate washstand was originally designed for a hairdressing salon. The taps/faucets are modern.

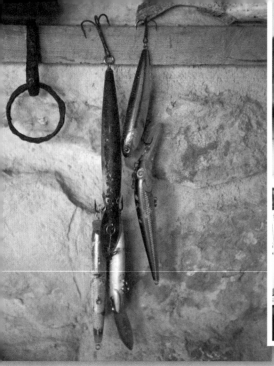

The former garage was transformed into a kitchen and open-plan living and dining room, and an upper level was installed to accommodate two bedrooms and a bathroom. The Madecs' daughter Charlotte has a bedroom and bathroom on the lower level. The kitchen floor and the work surfaces are covered in old slates salvaged from Serge's family home in Brittany.

In keeping with the agricultural aesthetic of the property, many of the original stone walls have been left exposed, and both the main fireplaces – those in the kitchen and in the living room – have been created from recycled materials. The flooring throughout the living areas consists of rustic wide oak planks.

ABOVE, LEFT TO RIGHT
Fisherman's lures, shells, pebbles and a collection of intriguing driftwood sculptures are just a few of the many items that recall the pleasure of walks on the beach all year round. Even in winter, there is much to delight the senses in Ile de Ré.
BELOW, LEFT TO RIGHT Both inside and outside their atmospheric house, the Madecs take pride

in displaying beautiful objects. This collection of candlesticks with metallic bases, a speckled model of a boat carved from driftwood and some boldly shaped 18th-century jars are just a few of their treasures.
OPPOSITE The Madecs' daughter Charlotte has a bedroom that looks out on the courtyard, where a profusion of lavenders jostles for space with the abundant vine.

Country kitchens

Given the French passion for food, it is not surprising that in most rural dwellings the kitchen is the heart of the home. Occupying centre stage is a large table made of scrubbed deal or pine, where food is prepared and also, more than likely, where it is eaten. Chairs are traditional in style, perhaps with rush or cane seats and ladderbacks. The freestanding design of many kitchens gives them an organic feel, as if the objects and appliances were growing naturally out of their surroundings.

The essence of a French country kitchen is its equipment. Rather than being hidden away, the pots and pans, knives, chopping boards and mixing bowls that make up the *batterie de cuisine* are displayed on open shelves. These often well-worn items are made from natural materials such as stoneware, wood and terracotta.

Dishes and utensils may be stored in an armoire – the large wooden cupboard, originally used as a linen store, found in nearly every French country home. Glazed doors or doors with chicken-wire panels allow the contents to be kept in view. Among other storage options is the ubiquitous *buffet*, or low sideboard.

The sink is usually made of stone or ceramic and set into a wooden surface, with cupboards or open shelves beneath it. Objects and the food itself add colour. There will be rich tones of French pottery, woven baskets and metalwork, sometimes polished copper and brass, but above all there will be fruit and herbs, bread and wine.

Lamb flavoured with a combination of anchovies and garlic is a long-established favourite of the Gascony area of south-west France, which is also renowned for its foie gras, truffles and high-quality charcuterie. According to the *gasconnade* method, the slow cooking in wine mellows the anchovies, making for a rich sauce and very tender meat. Serve with tagliatelle, potatoes or flageolet beans.

Agneau à la Gasconnade

1 leg of lamb (1.5 kg/
   3¼ lbs.), trimmed
14 canned anchovy fillets
2 tablespoons olive oil
2 onions, chopped
2 carrots, chopped
3 garlic cloves, crushed
2 tomatoes, skinned, seeded
   and chopped
750 ml/3 cups red wine
2 sprigs of thyme
1 fresh bay leaf
1 tablespoon tomato
   purée/paste
coarse sea salt

serves 4–6

Preheat the oven to 180°C (350°F) Gas 4.

Make slits all over the lamb and insert the anchovy fillets.

Heat the oil in a large flameproof casserole dish. Add the lamb and brown on all sides. Remove, season lightly with salt and set aside.

Put the onions and carrots in the casserole and cook over high heat for 3–5 minutes, until lightly browned. Add the garlic and chopped tomatoes and cook for 1 minute. Add the wine, thyme, bay leaf and tomato purée/paste and bring to the boil. Boil for 1 minute, then add the lamb.

Cover with the lid, transfer to the preheated oven and cook for 1½ hours, turning every 20 minutes or so. Remove the thyme and bay leaf and serve with the accompaniment of your choice.

LEFT In the entrance hall and the rooms on either side is an ancient tiled floor that has been preserved over the years with beeswax polish. The freestanding wooden shelves came from the village bakery. Above them is a painting of La Rochelle, where Mathilde's parents were born.
BELOW When placed in front of a vintage mirror, a pair of pink dahlias makes double the impact. The hand-blown vase is part of a collection of small items that are available for sale.

A repository of dreams

Furniture designer Mathilde Labrouche has created a beautiful home in Haute-Saintonge, an important wine-producing and agricultural region whose name means 'land of dreams'. Mathilde's little piece of dreamland is in the tiny hamlet of Chez Douteau, part of the commune of Messac, about 60 km (40 miles) north of Bordeaux. It is a long, narrow farmhouse with symmetrical doors and windows that typifies the architectural style of the region. She shares it with her son Pablo, her daughter Rosa, a dog, a cat and two chickens.

THIS PAGE Mathilde's talent for creating beautiful furniture from salvaged items is revealed in this unique table. The shapely stone legs have seen earlier service in an outdoor setting, perhaps as supports for flowerpots. The surface consists of several old beams cut to size, fitted together and inlaid with terracotta tiles.

THIS PICTURE On the kitchen mantelpiece is a group of exotic objects, dominated by an engraving of monkeys and framed specimens of insects and butterflies. Necklaces – mementoes of trips abroad – hang from a hook that once formed part of a gun rack. **BELOW** A view through the enfilade of bedrooms could almost be an illusion created by mirrors.

When Mathilde moved to Messac in 2005, it was a sad homecoming. She had been living with her husband and children in Bordeaux, when her husband died suddenly in an accident. Soon afterwards, Mathilde decided to return to the village of her birth, and to the house that her parents had bought more than a decade earlier as a holiday retreat. 'When we moved here, the living conditions were rudimentary,' explains Mathilde. 'I'd only ever visited the place in summer, and I hadn't realized that the wood fire was the only source of heating. There wasn't even a supply of hot water.'

Much of the modernization work was carried out by skilled local artisans, who took great care to respect the proportions of the original 18th-century building. Existing floors and structural materials – principally blocks of local limestone – were preserved, as were terracotta floor tiles and roof tiles. Most of the materials and the colours in place when Mathilde moved to the house have been retained.

THIS PAGE As in other spaces furnished by Mathilde, the bathrooms feature a seemingly artless integration of found, restored and contemporary objects. These range from a marble sink from Turkey teamed with a modern tap/faucet (left) to an old zinc basin placed on a slab of marble supported by wooden staircase balusters (below). The interior of the outdoor wetroom is reflected in a collection of assorted mirrors (bottom).

As a furniture designer, Mathilde specializes in creating beautiful new pieces from reclaimed materials, such as old wood, mirrors and textiles. Her early success led her to open two shops, in Ile de Ré and Bordeaux, and she has now transformed part of her home at Chez Douteau into a showroom, where she welcomes potential clients. There are examples of her work throughout the house.

Somewhat surprisingly, the builders' first task was to create an outdoor shower area – a luxury that Mathilde could not resist. This was followed by a complete renovation of the ground floor, which was designed to maintain the integrity of the original rooms and their original functions. The final stage was to update the first-floor bedrooms and bathroom. 'To me, this place is charged with a special energy as well as a natural beauty,' says Mathilde. 'The challenge was to find a style of decoration that would not destroy the atmosphere.'

THIS PAGE Occupying pride of place along one wall of the kitchen is this venerable chest, rescued from a service garage. It has been left in its original state, and some of the labels on the drawers have survived. The piece of broken panelling at the back was transformed into a naïve work of art by Mathilde's young son Pablo.

ABOVE The farmhouse table and mismatched chairs in the kitchen were picked up at various antiques markets and all of them have an intriguing history. The two chairs with carved backs are American – they were left behind in France by US soldiers after the Second World War. The eclectic mix of pots and pans, china and glass on the open shelves reflects Mathilde's love of spontaneity and disdain for formal arrangements.

The entrance remains just as it was when Mathilde arrived, with terracotta tiles on the floor, a vintage stone sink and original wooden shelves. Likewise, the basic elements of the kitchen – the floor, cupboards, walls and chimney – have been left exactly as they were. 'I made my own work surface in the kitchen, and brought in pieces of salvaged furniture, such as printer's chests,' she says. Freestanding modern appliances are located beside salvaged items, representing a pleasing rapport between old and new, decorative and practical. The dining area has been integrated into the kitchen, which Mathilde regards as a very important part of the house. 'We have slept in this kitchen over a long period,' she explains. 'My dream would be to put a bed back in there.'

The living room also retains many original features, including the floor and chimney, and is furnished with reclaimed pieces, as well as some of Mathilde's creations, including lamps and mirrors. More unusually, it also contains two beds. 'I love the idea of being able to sleep in places that were not intended for sleeping,' says Mathilde. Her mother helped to whitewash some walls and paint others in pigment colours such as pale ochre and sienna.

THIS PAGE Decorative simplicity is the guiding principle in the bedrooms. In some rooms, the only illumination is candlelight, but for her own bedroom (right) Mathilde created a lampshade from woollen threads found in Morocco. She used reclaimed wood to make the furniture in this room and the child's bedroom (above and top right).

ABOVE This outdoor wetroom in a former open-fronted barn was the first part of the house to be completed after Mathilde's arrival. Blurring the boundaries between inside and out, it is made entirely from recycled materials, such as floorboards and wooden panelling.

The large garden is enclosed by old barns that were originally used for crop storage and to shelter livestock. When Mathilde arrived, no flowers or shrubs had been planted here for many years, but she soon set about creating a *jardin de curé*, an old-fashioned priest's garden, which would once have been a source of food and medicinal herbs for the village priest, and also a place for reflection and meditation. 'I love old roses, poppies, wild irises,' says Mathilde. 'I have also devoted a part of the garden to traditional aromatic plants.'

The wines of Bordeaux

Bordeaux is the largest and most celebrated wine-producing region in the world. Although most of its wines are red (and known in Britain as 'claret'), some excellent dessert wines are also produced, and some fine dry whites. The region enjoys long hot summers followed by mild autumns, but its proximity to the Atlantic coast means that rain can fall at any time. The most important grapes are Merlot and Cabernet Sauvignon. Cabernet Franc is blended with both, adding complexity of flavour. Good red Bordeaux needs long ageing to reach its full potential.

The Bordeaux region occupies both sides of the Gironde River, whose main tributaries are the Dordogne and the Garonne. Grapes grown on the Left Bank of the Gironde, in places such as Pauillac, St Julien and Margaux, are dominated by the blackcurranty freshness and vigour of Cabernet Sauvignon. Those grown on the Right Bank – in Fronsac, Pomerol and St Emilion, for example – are softer, fuller and plummier, thanks to a higher proportion of Merlot.

Bordeaux's finest dry whites – blends of Sémillon and Sauvignon Blanc – originate in the gravel soils of Graves and Pessac-Léognan, at the southern end of the Left Bank. The sweet wines of Sauternes and Barsac are made from the same blend of grapes, but their vineyards are affected by noble rot (*Botrytis cinerea*). When it attacks ripe fruit, this fungal disease dehydrates the grapes while concentrating their flavours. The resulting wines, after a slow fermentation, are rich and luscious, with a wealth of flavour.

Although most of its wines are red, some excellent dessert wines are also produced, and some fine dry whites.

CHÂTEAU BE

DUBOIS-CHALLON

Premier Grand

Originating in the peasant cooking of the Limousin region of central France, *clafoutis* is now a popular dessert throughout France. Consisting of a custard-like batter usually baked with whole, stoned cherries, it is easy to cook. The only problem is the short length of the cherry season. Plums, pears and apples work well as substitutes, but rhubarb produces wonderful results – almost better than the original.

Clafoutis à la rhubarbe

500 g/1 lb. fresh rhubarb, trimmed and cut into 3-cm/1¼-inch slices
200 ml/¾ cup whole milk
200 ml/¾ cup double/heavy cream
3 medium/US large eggs
150 g/¾ cup sugar, plus extra for sprinkling
¼ teaspoon ground cinnamon
a pinch of salt
1 vanilla pod/bean, split lengthways with a small sharp knife
50 g/⅓ cup plain/all-purpose flour
butter, for greasing the dish

Serves 6

Preheat the oven to 200°C (400°F) Gas 6.

Bring a large saucepan of water to the boil, add the rhubarb and cook for 2 minutes, just to blanch. Drain and set aside.

Put the milk, cream, eggs, sugar, cinnamon and salt in a bowl and mix well. Using the tip of the knife, scrape the vanilla seeds from the pod/bean into the mixture. Add the flour and whisk well.

Grease a 30-cm/12-inch diameter baking dish with butter and sprinkle with sugar. Arrange the rhubarb in the dish. Pour the batter over the top and bake in the preheated oven for 40–45 minutes, until puffed and golden.

Une Terre d'Abondance

Midi-Pyrénées and Languedoc

4

Olives and olive oil

Olive oil has been treasured in Mediterranean countries for thousands of years and, as its health-promoting qualities become more widely acknowledged, it is now more popular than ever.

Production of olive oil in France is small compared to that of Spain and Italy, but an impressive array of olives is grown in Languedoc-Roussillon and Provence, and the broad range of tastes and styles – from light and fruity to rich and spicy – means there is something to suit every palate.

An impressive array of olives is grown in Languedoc-Roussillon and Provence, and the broad range of tastes and styles means there is something for every palate.

Most eating olives are picked from September onwards, when they are still green and not fully ripe, and some oils are made from this first picking. Among the distinctive eating varieties grown in Languedoc-Roussillon are Lucques and Picholine, while those used for oil include Aglandeau, Negrette and Rougette. As autumn progresses, the fruits still on the trees start to turn pale mauve and violet, eventually turning black when they are ready to be harvested for oil production.

All types of virgin and extra virgin oils are made from the first pressing of the olives. Chemicals and high heat are not allowed in the production of these oils, and no further processing or refining occurs after pressing is complete. Extra virgin olive oil must meet high aroma and flavour standards, as assessed by panels of experts, and contain no more than 0.8 per cent acidity. Although virgin olive oil is acceptable for cooking, extra virgin is much more desirable in salad dressings and as a dip for bread.

Widely regarded as one of the great Mediterranean dishes, *ratatouille* will perfume your kitchen with the essence of southern France. Cook each vegetable separately, and add the elements to the casserole in the order that best suits their cooking needs, before simmering them together. If you want the vegetables to keep their shape, cut the pieces medium-large, about 3–4 cm/1½ inches. *Ratatouille* can be eaten as an accompaniment to meat or on its own as an hors d'oeuvre. Serve with crusty bread.

Ratatouille

1 kg/2¼ lbs. aubergines/eggplants, cut into pieces

extra virgin olive oil

2 medium onions, coarsely chopped

2 red (bell) peppers, halved, seeded and cut into pieces

2 yellow (bell) peppers, halved, seeded and cut into pieces

1 green (bell) pepper, halved, seeded and cut into pieces

6 small courgettes/zucchini, about 750 g/1½ lbs., halved lengthways and sliced

5 garlic cloves, crushed

6 tomatoes, halved, seeded and chopped

leaves from a small bunch of basil, coarsely chopped, plus a few extra shredded

coarse sea salt

Serves 4–6

Put the aubergine/eggplant pieces in a microwave-proof bowl with 3 tablespoons water and microwave on high for 6 minutes. Drain and set aside.

Heat 3 tablespoons olive oil in a large flameproof casserole dish. Add the onions and cook for 3–5 minutes, until soft. Salt lightly.

Add the (bell) peppers and cook for 5–8 minutes, stirring often. Turn up the heat to keep the sizzling sound going, but take care not to let the vegetables burn. Salt lightly.

Add 1 more tablespoon olive oil and the courgettes/zucchini. Mix well and cook for about 5 minutes more, stirring occasionally. Salt lightly.

Add 2 more tablespoons olive oil and the drained aubergines/eggplants. Cook, stirring often, for 5 minutes more. Salt lightly.

Add 4 of the crushed garlic cloves and cook for 1 minute. Add 1 more tablespoon oil, if necessary, and the tomatoes and chopped basil and stir well. Salt lightly.

Cook for 5 minutes, then cover, reduce the heat and simmer gently for 30 minutes, checking occasionally.

Remove from the heat. Stir in the remaining garlic clove and shredded basil just before serving. Ratatouille is best served at room temperature, but it still tastes good hot. The longer you let it stand, the richer the flavour.

LEFT This sunny stairwell offers a warm welcome to guests. The contrast between the yellow on the upper walls and the grey below gives the entrance an even greater 'lift'.
BELOW Subtle use of earth colours, both inside and out, is one of the decorative triumphs at Les Sardines. Here, a pale terracotta pigment has been chosen for the exterior walls and a stone blue for woodwork.
BOTTOM The two-tone effect is evident in this interior corner, with soft apricot offsetting the rich chocolate tones.

Silk, sardines and ceramics

Anna Karin Punti and her husband Olivier moved to Gattigues, close to the ancient town of Uzès, in 2000. After a few years of living and working in Paris – she is a model and he a photographer – they had decided to change their lifestyle and open a guest house. It was a project that would allow them to spend more time with each other while raising a family. Their daughter, Clementine, is now eleven and their son, Nils, is six. They also share the house with three cats, who 'chose to live with us', says Anna Karin.

THIS PAGE An internal courtyard with plenty of greenery offers a cool retreat in the evenings and during the hottest part of the day. The sofa – a metal campaign bed, dressed with vintage textiles – and the elaborately framed mirror make it easy to mistake the courtyard for an ordinary room.

THIS PAGE The raw-plaster walls in this living-room corner and alcove complement the exposed stonework and enhance its cooling effect, as does the irregular terracotta-tiled floor. By contrast, the red and orange cushions introduce hot accents, enlivening a simple daybed, whose top can be lifted up to reveal a storage chest.

Anna Karin and Olivier first considered moving to an area nearer Paris, but couldn't find a property that was both desirable and affordable. Everything changed at the turn of the millennium, with the introduction of the high-speed TGV train service from Paris to Avignon, taking 2½ hours and making the South of France more accessible to visitors.

The couple bought a house in a hamlet of 80 people – one of five such hamlets that make up the local commune – just ten minutes' drive from Uzès and one hour away from Avignon. Other nearby attractions include the Pont du Gard, the spectacular three-tiered Roman aqueduct across the Gardon River, and the village of St-Quentin-la-Poterie, where you can visit working potteries and invest in some original ceramics.

With its oldest part dating from the 16th century, the house had new wings added in the 18th and 19th centuries. All the elements are made entirely of stone, with some walls or parts of walls covered in plaster and painted. The property's organic growth led to some architectural oddities. One window survives in an inside wall, for example, and there is an indoor well that used to be outside.

The house is a former *magnanerie*, or place where silk worms were farmed. This area of France was a vibrant centre of silk production in the 19th century, reflecting the importance of nearby Nîmes as a textile town. The first ever blue jeans came from Nîmes; indeed, the word 'denim' derives from the phrase '*de Nîmes*'.

When the Puntis acquired the property, it was a wreck. There was no plumbing, no electricity and no central heating. It had been lived in for decade by an elderly bachelor whose family had rented the property for four generations but made no improvements. Having obtained quotations from builders, the Puntis realized that they could not afford to pay someone else to do the renovation work, so Olivier decided to do it himself. He taught himself how to plumb, install electrical wiring, lay the concrete floors and put on a new roof.

ABOVE RIGHT A curvy armchair upholstered in bright red stands out boldly against the marble fireplace. Again, rough plaster has been used to create a rustic effect. The slim lampstands on the mantelpiece are reminiscent of crosses on an altar.
RIGHT Spiky branches in a florist's bucket have the perfect backdrop in a two-tone wall of earthy reds.

RIGHT The bands of colour in the minimalist artwork above the Swedish sofa-bed reflect the two-tone finish on the walls, where the darker shade – a charcoal grey – is painted up to dado height.

OPPOSITE The flamboyant lampshades in the master bedroom were created from bric-a-brac by the designer Richard Goullet. Real pebbles – reminding Anna Karin of Gothenburg – were inlaid into the floor by Olivier.

BELOW Furnishings in one of the guest bedrooms are almost austere, with a simple drop-leaf table flanked by a slatted bench and matching chair. Mauve and greyish blue are typical of the stone colours favoured by Anna Karin.

RIGHT AND FAR RIGHT White is the dominant colour in this bright and cheerful bathroom, where the walls are finished with varying widths of tongue-and-groove panelling and hung with antique mirrors, enhancing the country feel. The pair of round porcelain sinks on the tiled washstand recall the bowls and pitchers that were common before the advent of piped water. They make a perfect complement to the vintage freestanding bathtub and its diaphanous shower curtain.

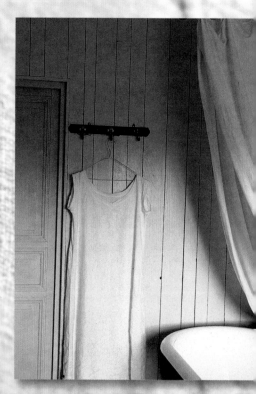

It was during the process of renovation that the property acquired its curious name of *Les Sardines aux Yeux Bleus* ('the sardines with blue eyes'.)'*Les Sardines*' comes from the emblem of a sardine that forms part of the traditional keyhole design that is found on many of the doors in the house, while '*aux Yeux Bleus*' is a reference to Anna Karin's Swedish origins.

Adjoining the family quarters is the guest house, consisting of three bedrooms and three apartments. The bedrooms are arranged around an internal courtyard and on the second floor there are two apartments, one large and one small. There is one more apartment in the garden in a former *maison de gardien* (caretaker's house).

When the building work was finished, the Puntis engaged the innovative interior decorator Richard Goullet,

whose first task was to paint the Rose Room. Under Richard's guidance, Anna Karin then took over responsibility for the practical decoration, starting with the Blue Room and the Green Room. Meanwhile, Richard was given three crates of bric-a-brac picked up at flea markets and *brocantes*, from which he made 17 lamps for the house.

The colours used in the interior betray a strong Scandinavian influence: stone and taupe, washed-out blues, dusky pinks and every shade of grey. Anna Karin comes originally from Gothenburg, a port city surrounded by a barren, rocky landscape. To help her feel at home, Olivier incorporated stones found on the beach in the concrete flooring. 'I grew up around water,' says Anna Karin and, even though she now lives quite a distance from the sea, she wants to recreate the feel of it in her living environment.

ABOVE Among several rooms shared by visitors to Les Sardines is a large kitchen with an old flagstone floor and a huge open fireplace that's kept well supplied with logs – perfect for slightly chilly evenings in autumn or early spring. In front of the fire is a simple, square table covered with a fresh white linen cloth and surrounded by a set of slatted garden chairs, flanked by a slender console table and a shelf lined with grassy green-glazed ceramics. Anna Karin and Olivier provide breakfast but no other meals, instead encouraging their guests to eat at one of the many local restaurants or to take advantage of the area's wonderful produce and concoct their own feasts.

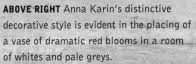

ABOVE RIGHT Anna Karin's distinctive decorative style is evident in the placing of a vase of dramatic red blooms in a room of whites and pale greys.

RIGHT This arched-topped front door is in one of the older parts of the house, which dates back to the 16th century. In the 19th century it flourished as a *magnanerie*, or silk farm.

Building materials

Wood and stone, often locally sourced, are highly prized in France as both exterior and interior building materials. Exterior wooden shutters, for example, are used all over the country – for aesthetic as well as practical reasons.

Wood panelling and detailing are seen in many French homes, and much built-in furniture is also wooden. Sturdy timber beams are sometimes left in their natural state but are more usually painted or colour-stained. Wooden floors can be stained, sealed and polished, waxed, limed or painted.

Stone is often used for walls and floors. Although new stone takes time to weather well, old stone has a softness and tonal variety that is immensely appealing. A particular joy is an interior cobblestone floor, where the rounded shape of each stone brings texture as well as a sculptural quality to the room.

Since clay is found throughout France, terracotta is ubiquitous, particularly in the form of floor tiles. Although strictly speaking a man-made material, terracotta has acquired credibility from its long history, dating back to the Romans. Both terracotta and its close companion brick are characterized by a sensuous warmth deriving from both colour and tactility. Smaller terracotta tiles are used for walls and surfaces.

A long-established affinity with metal is still evident in France. As well as occasional furniture, such as outdoor tables and chairs, metal is used to make window grilles, sinuous stair rails and banisters, kitchen fittings and door furniture.

Although new stone takes time to weather well, old stone has a softness and tonal variety that is immensely appealing.

Cassoulet is a hearty combination of beans baked with meats. Despite the long list of ingredients, it is not hard to cook, though you need to start preparations at least a day in advance of serving – and you will need several large pots and a large casserole dish to cook it in. Cook the beans, cook the meat stew, brown the duck and sausages, then put it all together: that's it. The sausages should have as high a pork content as possible. Duck confit is sold canned in large supermarkets and some delicatessens.

Cassoulet

850 g/1¾ lbs. dried haricot beans
300 g/10 oz. thick-sliced unsmoked middle bacon
rind from 4 thick pork chops or a piece of salt pork
1 carrot, chopped
1 fresh bay leaf
1 onion, studded with 2 cloves
4 whole garlic cloves, peeled
1 teaspoon salt

meat stew
1 tablespoon olive oil
750 g/1½ lbs. pork spare ribs
750 g/1½ lbs. boneless lamb shoulder, cubed
1 onion, chopped
3 garlic cloves, crushed
400 g/14 oz. canned chopped tomatoes
1 fresh bay leaf
2 litres/quarts fresh chicken stock
6 canned duck confit thigh pieces
10 Toulouse sausages or other pure pork sausages
150 g/3 cups fresh breadcrumbs
coarse sea salt and freshly ground black pepper

Serves 8

One day before serving, in the morning, put the beans in a bowl with plenty of cold water and let soak. (Soak for at least 6 hours, or start 2 days early and soak overnight.)

Drain the beans. Put in a large saucepan with cold water to cover, bring to the boil and simmer for 10 minutes. Drain. Return the beans to the pan and add the bacon, pork rind or salt pork, carrot, bay leaf, onion and garlic. Cover with water by about 5 cm/2 inches and bring to the boil. Lower the heat and simmer gently for 1 hour.

Add 1 teaspoon salt and continue cooking for 30 minutes more. Let cool, then refrigerate overnight; do not drain.

Meanwhile, to prepare the meat stew, heat the oil in a large frying pan. Add the pork and lamb and fry until brown. Add the onion and garlic and cook for about 3 minutes, until just soft. Add the tomatoes, bay leaf and stock. Season. Bring to the boil and skim off the foam, then lower the heat, cover and simmer gently for 1½ hours. Add salt and pepper to taste. Let cool, cover and refrigerate overnight.

The next day, about 3 hours before serving, discard the fat from the top of the stew. Remove the meat from the spare ribs, return it to the stew and discard the bones.

Bring the beans to room temperature (or warm slightly), drain and reserve the liquid. Season to taste.

Heat a large frying pan, add the duck confit pieces and fry until browned. Remove, cut the thighs into pieces and set aside. In the same pan, brown the sausages. Do not discard the cooking fat.

Preheat the oven to 220°C (425°F) Gas 7. Remove the pork rind or salt pork and bacon from the beans and put it in a casserole dish. Top with one-third of the beans. Arrange the duck confit in the middle and the sausages around the edge. Spread the meat stew on top. Cover with the remaining beans. Spoon in some of the reserved bean liquid (you should just be able to see it), then sprinkle with a thin layer of breadcrumbs. Pour in the duck and sausage fat. Cook in the preheated oven for 30 minutes.

Reduce the oven temperature to 190°C (375°F) Gas 5. Gently break up the crust on top, then spoon over some more bean liquid and sprinkle with more breadcrumbs. Continue checking, about every 30 minutes or so, adding more liquid as necessary; be careful not to let the cassoulet dry out. When the cassoulet has cooked for 2 hours and the crust is well browned, remove from the oven and serve.

Roquefort cheese

Within easy reach of the spectacular Gorges du Tarn and the Millau viaduct, a marvel of modern engineering, is the small village of Roquefort-sur-Soulzon, where the fabulous blue cheese known as Roquefort has been produced since Roman times.

Noted for its sharp, tangy, salty flavour and its rich, creamy texture, Roquefort is made primarily from the milk of the Lacaune sheep that graze the nearby Larzac plateau. It is matured for three months in the chilly, damp caves at Combalou, where the mould that gives the cheese its distinctive character is found in the soil. Traditionally, bread was left in the caves for six to eight weeks until it was consumed by the mould, then dried to produce a powder. Today, the mould can be grown in a laboratory.

Legend has it that the cheese was discovered when a youth, eating his lunch of bread and ewes' milk cheese, saw a beautiful girl in the distance. Abandoning his meal in a nearby cave, he ran to meet her. When he returned – a few months later – the mould had transformed his plain cheese into Roquefort.

In 1925 Roquefort was granted France's first *Appellation d'Origine Contrôlée* (AOC), when regulations controlling its production and naming were defined. In 1961 it was decreed that, although the method for making the cheese could be followed across the South of France, only those 'wheels' whose ripening occurred in the Combalou caves were permitted to bear the name Roquefort. Annual production now reaches about 19,000 tonnes.

The French have always flattered
themselves that they have gone
further in the art of living, in what
they call l'entente de la vie, than
any other people, and with certain
restrictions the claim is just.

Henry James

The French have always flattered

themselves that they have gone

further in the art of living, in what

they call l'entente de la vie, than

any other people, and with certain

restrictions the claim is just.

Henry James

A haven of curiosities

The beautiful city of Nîmes, capital of the Gard department of Languedoc–Roussillon, has many fascinating reminders of its heyday during the Roman Empire, when it was a key staging post on the Via Domitia, the ancient Roman road linking Italy with Spain. The city's emblem is a crocodile chained to a palm tree, symbolizing the Roman conquest of Egypt.

LEFT The exotic contents of this Nîmes apartment reflect the rich history of its location at a crossroads of the Roman Empire. In the living room, an interesting mix of classical and religious objects is overlooked by a faded fresco-style painting of a biblical scene.

ABOVE Crocodile images can be seen all over the city of Nîmes – reminders of the Roman conquest of Egypt in 30 BC.

LEFT AND ABOVE The walls of the study are painted a brilliant blue, reminiscent of an artistic rendering of the Virgin Mary's veil. They provide a wonderful backdrop for an eclectic collection of furniture, including a 1850s English mahogany tallboy and a red velvet *lit de repos* from the era of Louis XVI (1774–92).

BELOW LEFT A goldfinch whose song mimics the ringing of the front doorbell is the proud inhabitant of the elaborate Indian birdcage in the dining room.
OPPOSITE Guarded by a fierce African mask, this corner of the living room with its long, narrow beech table has been appropriated by Matthieu as a spot for work and study.

Just north of the spectacular Arena, still a vibrant venue for live entertainments, is the place du Marché, where Jean-Louis Fages runs a shop selling antiques and homewares, including made-to-measure lampshades. A native of Nîmes, Jean-Louis opened his first antiques shop in the city more than 30 years ago. The present one, aptly named Le Cabinet des Curiosités, is full of reproductions of his favourite styles, primarily from the 18th century.

Jean-Louis and his partner Matthieu share a love of collecting, and the two of them often go searching for treasures to fill their elegant Nîmes home – which, just like the shop, is an emporium of curiosities. The pair's eclectic taste is evident from the décor and furnishings of the apartment, located on the top floor of an 1830s building overlooking the Maison Carrée, an astonishingly well-preserved Roman temple set in the middle of a huge square.

Jean-Louis and Matthieu have transformed their apartment from the bland, featureless box they found when they first entered the building a decade ago. High double doors swing open to reveal a small black-and-white tiled hallway, beyond which is the main salon or living room.

All the rooms, which lead off one another, have floor-to-ceiling French windows that open onto a balcony encircling the apartment and flood the interior with natural light.

Artificial lighting has been carefully chosen and imaginatively positioned. While lamps are generally traditional in style, each lampshade has its own distinctive character and is used to enhance and complement the surrounding décor. Table lights and chandeliers are controlled by dimmer switches, while candlelight plays an important part in creating an intimate atmosphere.

The salon is dominated by a trompe l'oeil cityscape framed by chunky ceramic lamps and silver candlesticks. The statuettes in this room look as if they could have come straight out of the painting. In another exotic touch, a leopard skin has been draped over the back of a curvaceous sofa and complemented with a 19th-century Moroccan kilim and some brightly patterned cushion covers.

Matthieu, a lawyer who often works from home, has made a desk from the narrow beech dining table backed by floor-to-ceiling shelves and cupboards. Such storage, either freestanding or built in, is a feature of several rooms in the apartment, and is used to house everything from books and photographs to glassware, china and vases.

Leading off the salon is the study, where vibrant blue walls make a wonderful backdrop for some 18th-century English mahogany pieces and a red velvet daybed. Next comes the dining room, where the dominant colour is apple green, offsetting furniture in a mixture of styles and epochs, including an English mahogany pedestal dining table, a modern console table and a French crystal chandelier.

The compact kitchen is enlivened by a collection of 19th-century apothecary jars, marble mortars and pestles and white ceramic confit jars. Not simply for display, these objects are in everyday use in the creation of great meals.

OPPOSITE AND ABOVE RIGHT
A refreshing apple green is the dominant colour in the dining room. Someone with a talented artistic eye has clearly influenced the display of objects in this room – not only the paintings and engravings on the walls, but also the plates and cutlery/flatware on the table; even the arrangement of fruit and nuts resembles a classical still life.

RIGHT The kitchen is very much a working room with just enough space to squeeze in a small bistro table and two chairs. Small round spice pots are attached to the wall by magnets on their bases, which means that they can be moved around to create varying geometric patterns. Just visible at the top of the picture is a 17th-century Dutch chandelier – a treasured family heirloom.

France is the largest apricot producer in Europe, with some 30 varieties to choose from. The fruits are harvested from early to late summer, depending on species and region. Apricots can be eaten fresh, stewed or made into jam, but there is no better way to enjoy them than baked in a tart. This version requires little effort to prepare. Red plums, nectarines or peaches can be used in place of apricots.

Tarte aux abricots

375 g/13 oz. ready-rolled
 puff pastry, chilled
1 egg, beaten, for glazing
500 g/1 lb. ripe apricots,
 halved and stoned/pitted,
 the stones/pits reserved
100 g/⅓ cup apricot jam
1 tablespoon freshly
 squeezed lemon juice
4 tablespoons vanilla sugar
sifted icing/confectioners'
 sugar, to decorate
 (optional)

Serves 4–6

Unroll the pastry and cut out a circle 25 cm/10 inches in diameter. Re-roll the offcuts and make 4 strips about 2 x 25 cm/¾ x 10 inches. Set aside.

Transfer the pastry to a lightly oiled baking sheet. Leaving a 2-cm/½-inch border all round, prick the rest of the pastry with a fork.

Preheat the oven to 220°C (425°F) Gas 7.

Brush the unpricked border of the pastry with the beaten egg. Place the pastry strips on it, cutting the ends to be joined on the diagonal and pressing them neatly together. These will puff up when baked, and act like a wall around the fruit.

Brush beaten egg all over the pastry, including the pricked area. Blind bake for 20 minutes, or until golden and risen at the edges. Prick once again.

Meanwhile, crack open 6 of the apricot stones/pits. Remove and shred the kernels. Cut each apricot half into 6 segments. Arrange them, flesh upwards, on the pastry. Scatter the shredded kernels over the top.

Put the jam and lemon juice in a small bowl and stir until smooth. Using a pastry brush, paint this glaze all over the fruit.

Sprinkle on the vanilla sugar, then bake for 20 minutes, until the apricots are soft, fragrant and slightly browned at the tips. Serve warm, dusted with icing/confectioners' sugar, if liked.

Beautiful fabrics

France has led the way in textile design since the 17th century, when the French East India Company imported calicos and chintzes printed with floral and geometric motifs. Known as Indiennes after their land of origin, they were hugely popular, and seen as a threat to the Lyons silk-weaving industry – so a 50-year ban was imposed on the manufacture or sale of all printed cottons.

In 1760, after the ban was lifted, Christophe-Philippe Oberkampf opened a cotton-printing works at Jouy-en-Josas, south-west of Paris, and hired the talented designer Christophe Huet. They produced not only Indiennes but also toiles de Jouy, cotton fabrics printed with pictorial designs, often of pastoral scenes, flower arrangements or chinoiserie fantasies. Now seen on everything from curtains to quilts, in faded hues of rose madder and indigo or vibrant shades of orange and yellow, toiles de Jouy instantly evoke the essence of a French interior.

Two types of stripe predominate in French fabric design: traditional mattress ticking, and a design incorporating stripes of different widths in combinations of blue, buff, pink and cream.

Traditional quilts known as *boutis* are widely used on beds, as throws and covers on sofas and chairs, and as tablecloths. Antique *boutis*, sometimes embellished with elaborate stitching, are avidly collected today, but new ones, in the same soft colour combinations, can also be found.

Old linen sheets, particularly when monogrammed and embroidered, are commonly recycled as bed covers, tablecloths and lightweight curtains.

Toiles de Jouy are cotton
fabrics printed with pictorial
designs, often of pastoral
scenes, flowers or
chinoiserie fantasies.

Une Fête de Sens

Provence and the Cote D'Azur

Outdoor living

The climate of southern France is wonderfully conducive to open-air living, but the strength of the summer sun means that every outside living area should include a shady retreat. This can take many forms – a porch attached to the house, a vine-covered pergola, a terrace with an awning or a tree-dappled corner of the garden.

An outdoor room, however simple, should be practical and comfortable in all its aspects, and adorned by beautiful objects. Antique wrought-iron tables, chairs and benches are particularly sought after. Wooden tables and chairs are either stained or left to age gently; wicker and cane chairs are often painted in greys, blues and greens, and then allowed to weather and fade. Seat cushions in all shapes and sizes, covered in striped and checked designs or pretty floral prints, add comfort and vibrancy to the scene.

Alfresco meals offer the ideal opportunity for a range of aesthetic pleasures. Tablecloths, napkins and fresh flowers can transform the table into a work of art, and food served in wooden and terracotta dishes will enhance the rustic feel. Plates and glasses should be simple and sturdy, and complemented by piles of coloured pottery.

Plant containers are an important element of every outdoor space. In Provence, hand-thrown terracotta flowerpots and stone urns are the most popular varieties. Wooden containers are likely to be either the straight-sided type known as Versailles pots or curved tub shapes.

We have come five hundred miles by rail through the heart of France. What a bewitching land it is! What a garden! All is orderly and beautiful – everything is charming to the eye.

Mark Twain

"We have come five hundred miles by rail through the heart of France. What a beautiful land it is! What a garden! All is orderly and beautiful — everything is charming to the eye.

Mark Twain

A nostalgic recreation

Midway between the Cévennes National Park and the marshy Camargue, two of the natural wonders of France, stands an extraordinary house with an extraordinary history. Dating from the 16th century, the chateau de Christin was built in an architectural style that recalls the Doge's Palace in Venice. Its front façade has a dramatic sweeping rooftop in the shape of a coronet. The restored chateau is now run as a hotel by Nina and Olivier Delafargue, who moved there to escape the urban jungle of Marseilles, where they had worked for many years.

ABOVE The earliest part of the chateau de Christin dates from the 16th century.
RIGHT In an annexe to the entrance hall is a majestic stone fireplace with a bread oven at one end, suggesting that it was the original kitchen range. No longer used for cooking, the fireplace accommodates a roaring log fire in winter.

The Delafargues bought the house in 2007 from the famous decorator Jean-Loup Daraux, who had overseen its renovation to 18th-century glory by a team of skilled craftsmen and artists. Among the many restored elements are box ceilings, cornices and wall mouldings, many square metres of wood panelling, floor tiles and exquisitely decorated cupboards and doors. In the private quarters on the upper floor are quatrefoil windows in the Gothic style.

As well as making a comfortable home for themselves, Nina and Olivier decided to open the house to discriminating visitors seeking a respite from city life. There are 18 rooms in the main building, and the former

OPPOSITE Scenes of local rural life adorn the walls in the main dining room, while cleverly concealed within the beautiful panelling is a secret door to the kitchen. The ivory-handled forks hanging from the chandelier were added by Richard Goullet.

ABOVE AND LEFT Every room has something to intrigue the visitor. The small dining room (above) includes an unusual Comtoise clock with a distinctive potbellied case, while the hall is graced with a 19th-century birdcage, home to a pair of stone chickens.

LEFT In a corner of Nina and Olivier's bedroom, a 19th-century *fauteuil* covered in reproduction toile de Jouy stands in front of a quatrefoil window.
ABOVE Frescoes are one of the many forms of artistry that give this house its special character. Here, a floral theme has been chosen to enliven a monastic-style bedroom.
BELOW Posters above a mahogany daybed give a hint of what's to come in the Herbalist's Suite – through the double doors – where all the decorative elements reflect a botanical theme.
OPPOSITE Former stables have been converted into a vast upstairs salon, whose centrepiece is this simple stone fireplace.

stable block has also been converted into a separate house for a large group. Evident throughout the chateau is the Delafargues' love of antiques, from simple garden benches and hunting trophies to antique crystal chandeliers and rococo mirrors. Trompe l'oeil paintings and fresco-style illustrations adorn many of the walls. One panel in the dining room is decorated with a scene of the nearby Camargue, where herds of white horses gallop free.

Nina and Olivier asked the designer Richard Goullet, a close friend, to add his distinctive touches to the decorative scheme. Among Richard's contributions was to mix *chaux* (limewash) to the right shade of pink for the couple's bedroom, so that it matched exactly the colour of the old rose 'Pierre de Ronsard' growing outside. He also added a set of tiny ivory-handled forks to an icicle-drop chandelier.

A grand staircase sweeps up from the terrazzo floor in the hallway to the five elegant and individual guest bedrooms. Each of the rooms has its own distinct character. The *Suite de l'Herboriste* is lined with old prints of plants, leaves and seeds. The *Chambre Bleu*, on the garden side of the building, contains decorative elements and objects in myriad shades of blue. The *Chambre de Marquis* – a reference to the building's very first owner – has highly ornate

furniture and a stuccoed ceiling. And, as you would expect, birds and tulips respectively adorn the walls in the *Chambre des Oiseaux* and the *Chambre aux Tulipes*.

The spectacular terraced gardens that surround the chateau include an olive grove with a large pond and stone statues, a potager and a rose-covered walkway. The pool area, concealed by a neatly clipped box hedge, offers breathtaking views over the nearby countryside.

ABOVE This slightly ramshackle potager – a vegetable garden incorporating flowers and shrubs – makes up just a small section of the chateau grounds. Its sheltered seating area offers a relaxed retreat from the formal terraced gardens, which are carefully delineated by rows of box hedges and topiary balls, gravel paths and walkways.

ABOVE The enormous glazed terracotta pots flanking the entrance, made in the nearby village of Anduze, represent a style of container seen all over the South of France. The resident collie, Avrile, has witnessed the transformation of the chateau from start to finish. She was 14 years old when this photograph was taken.
LEFT When the weather is fine, Nina and Olivier prefer to take their meals outside the kitchen in this sheltered terraced seating area, which is also used for repotting plants and flower arranging. The sturdy teak fold-up dining chairs have weathered many a summer.

2 litres/quarts boiling water
1 fresh bouquet garni:
 parsley, thyme, celery
 and bay, tied together
250 g/9 oz. pumpkin,
 marrow, squash or sweet
 potato, seeded, peeled
 and cubed
200 g/7 oz. fresh coco beans
 or equivalent
2 carrots, sliced
2 onions, sliced
200 g/7 oz. small potatoes,
 peeled and quartered
200 g/7 oz. green beans,
 such as haricot or
 runner/string beans,
 cut into 10-cm/
 4-inch pieces
2 medium courgettes/
 zucchini, sliced
a handful of broken
 spaghetti, vermicelli
 or short macaroni
2 tomatoes, blanched,
 peeled and cubed

pistou

1 teaspoon rock salt
freshly ground black pepper
6 young garlic cloves,
 chopped
a handful of basil leaves
 and basil buds, torn
50 g/½ cup grated
 Parmesan or pecorino
 cheese
25 g/¼ cup grated tomme
 de chèvre (hard goat
 cheese)
150 ml/⅔ cup extra virgin
 olive oil

Serves 4–6

This satisfying vegetable soup is enriched with pistou – a paste of garlic, basil, cheese and olive oil. (The word *pistou* comes from 'pestle', the pounding tool from which it is traditionally made.) The original version of the soup was thick and plain, containing only potatoes, beans, tomatoes and pasta. Today, most Provençal cooks add several kinds of bean, plus courgettes/zucchini, carrots and onion. Freshly podded coco beans are a favourite ingredient, but fresh or canned white haricot, cannellini or butter/lima beans can be used instead. Serve with crusty bread.

Soupe au pistou

Pour the boiling water into a large soup pan. Add the bouquet garni, pumpkin, beans, carrots, onions and potatoes, and return to the boil. Reduce the heat to a moderate simmer, then cover and cook for 20 minutes.

Add the green beans, courgettes/zucchini, pasta and tomatoes. Continue cooking for 10 minutes, until the vegetables and pasta are soft.

Meanwhile, make the pistou. Put the salt, pepper, garlic and basil into a mortar and pound to a paste with a pestle. Add some of the cheese and a splash of the olive oil, and pound until a stiff paste forms. Continue adding the remaining cheese and oil, pounding each addition. The final paste should be thick and rich.

Ladle the soup into big, individual bowls and let diners stir in their own pistou as they eat.

RIGHT AND BELOW The salient feature of the internal organization of this light-filled house is that all the main living zones flow into each other – without, apparently, the impediment of walls or doors. The sense of space is enhanced by the liberal use of white paint and white fabric, as well as an abundance of mirrors. In some cases, mirrors are reflected within mirrors.

BELOW RIGHT The juxtaposition of contrasting textures adds visual and tactile interest to what might otherwise have turned out to be a rather bland interior scheme.

A spiritual retreat

This simple rustic house near the village of Lourmarin in the southern Luberon has been transformed into a positive haven of tranquillity by its inspired and inspirational owners, Bruno and Michèle Viard. Familiar with the Luberon area from childhood, the pair have restored and extended the 19th-century house with the greatest of care, always respecting the traditional styles of the region.

THIS PAGE An enigmatic oil painting of a musician, its details worn away by time, is one of the few pieces of wall art that has been allowed into the house. The portrait's golden bronze tints are reflected in the row of tin trays underneath. The polished concrete floor is an important factor in helping to unify the disparate living spaces.

Michèle's motivation has been to create calm, free-flowing spaces featuring an abundance of light. For most of the time, she and Bruno live in Marseilles, where Michèle is a teacher of Latin and Greek, but this charming holiday home has allowed her to indulge her instinctive love of architecture, especially interior architecture, and experiment with its psychological effects.

Michèle acknowledges the influence of the Japanese architect Tadao Ando and the Mexican master of space and light Luis Barragán. She believes that simplicity and serenity have a hugely beneficial effect on wellbeing.

After buying the house in 1975, Michèle and Bruno carried out some small-scale alterations themselves, but they hired an architect for the big projects. The change was slow and organic. Even today, according to Michèle, the house is in a state of constant evolution. 'When I get a good idea, I like to try it out. Of course, it's a process of trial and error,' she says. 'Many things have changed over the years, but the spirit of the place has been preserved.'

Viewed from the outside, the building has retained a strong sense of integrity. The meticulous choice of materials and the natural ageing process have made it impossible to distinguish between the original walls and the additions. Almost all the windows are still their original size, with the exception of a wide bay in the new part of the house, which resembles a large studio window. Wooden window frames have been replaced by slim metal frames that allow more light to penetrate into the interior.

The beams and other old materials came from salvage yards, while bathroom fixtures and decorative elements were picked up in local antiques shops or serendipitously discovered during Bruno and Michèle's travels. Certain details – such as the insertion into the walls of hanging rods that resemble coat pegs – reflect regional customs. Similarly, the use of polished concrete flooring is a new interpretation of the more traditional terracotta floor tiles.

The entrance is through an enclosed courtyard that gives access to the kitchen and, beyond that, to the dining room and living room. All the rooms on the ground floor flow into each other, united by the concrete floor. Natural materials such as wood and stone predominate – limewashed, painted white or, where possible, used in a simple, unadorned state. Contrasted with this simplicity, the occasional dramatic piece such as an enigmatic oil painting or a mirror with a baroque frame makes a strong impact. Mirrors are used all over the house to reflect light and make spaces seem bigger.

Evident also in every room is a combination of vintage and modern items – in the dining room, for example, is an antique wooden dining table flanked by a set of plastic designer chairs. Michèle strives to establish a good balance between old and new, since, she believes, each softens the effect of the other, and the mix has a calming influence

OPPOSITE ABOVE LEFT Most of the white beams in the house were retrieved from salvage yards.

OPPOSITE ABOVE RIGHT When the decorative approach is so sparse, even the simplest displays can have a strong impact.

OPPOSITE BELOW LEFT Painting the wall grey to waist height, so that it matches the colour of the concrete floor, reduces the starkness of the white walls, making the space seem cosier.

OPPOSITE BELOW RIGHT The bathroom surfaces are made of solid concrete, but the effect is lightened by an old-fashioned mirror and chandelier.

THIS PAGE Stone steps lead down to a guest bedroom that can be isolated from the rest of the house if its occupant is in need of privacy. The most dramatic item in this room is the ornate rococo headboard.

because it reflects the rhythms of real life. 'If such a profession existed, you would be a "space therapist",' a friend once told her.

On the first floor, there is a one double bedroom and two smaller bedrooms. At the back is a large bedroom and bathroom with a separate entrance – this can be closed off from the rest of the house for privacy or solitude. Again, simplicity and serenity are the defining characteristics of the décor in these spaces. A former chapel in the grounds has been converted into an additional guest bedroom and bathroom.

A garden of 3 hectares (7½ acres) surrounds the house, offering spectacular views of the mountains. In the grounds are about 400 olive trees, planted by Bruno in 2001 and since tended by Michèle, which now yield a bounteous supply of olive oil and olives for eating. The property also supports pines, oaks, vines and a variety of fruit trees including cherries and apricots.

Lavender fields

Carpets of deep-mauve or violet-blue flowers stretching towards the horizon symbolize for many people the very essence of Provence. Lavender fields also shape the character of the landscape – even local shutters are painted in lavender colours.

Wild outcrops of true lavender (*Lavandula angustifolia*) have flourished for centuries on the slopes of Mount Ventoux, but cultivated varieties, mainly *Lavandula latifolia*, a hybrid, are now the mainstay of local production. The plants still thrive on the high plateaux in the Sault area, at the base of Mount Ventoux, as well as growing in abundance in the Luberon and the Valréas regions.

Lavender blooms from late June to August. The crop is at its most intoxicating in mid-July, when the buds burst open and the scent is released. Harvest then happens quickly and the distillation process begins. The finished product ends up in oils, perfumes, cosmetics and soaps. Summer festivals in towns and villages act as a showcase for local produce, including lavender honey and dried-flower arrangements.

Provençal lavender thrives as a perennial in arid climates. It can be planted in open fields, in herb gardens, as a border for flower beds, as added colour and fragrance along a walkway or garden path or in patio containers.

Lavender is said to heal insect bites and burns as well as repel insects. It soothes headaches if applied to the temples, and can be used as an aid to sleep.

The lavender crop is at its most intoxicating in mid-July, when the buds burst open and the scent is released.

Reminiscent of lazy summer lunches overlooking the Mediterranean, this crisp salad can be made in various different ways. According to some, the essential ingredients are tuna, anchovies, tomatoes, potatoes, French beans, hard-boiled eggs and lettuce. Others say that it must include cucumber, green (bell) pepper, spring onions, raw broad/fava beans and basil leaves, while tender baby artichokes, ideally raw, are desirable. Black olives are usual. This recipe follows the second group – who also argue that no cooked vegetables are allowed.

Salade Niçoise

2 garlic cloves, lightly crushed and halved

1 head of cos/romaine lettuce, or ½ head of Batavia or frisée

1 small gem/Boston lettuce or other crisp baby lettuce (optional)

2 spring onions/scallions, sliced

250–350 g/9–12 oz. good-quality canned tuna pieces or cooked, cold fresh tuna

50 g/2 oz. salted anchovies or 24 canned anchovy fillets

24 black olives, Niçoise type

3 or 4 hard-boiled eggs, shelled and halved or quartered

a handful of small basil leaves, roughly torn

200 g/7 oz. fresh broad/fava beans, podded and peeled

2 ripe red tomatoes, each cut into 6 or 8 wedges

10-cm/4-inch piece of cucumber, peeled and cubed

2 fresh baby artichokes, trimmed, halved and chokes removed (or canned equivalent)

4 radishes, sliced

8 tablespoons extra virgin olive oil

½ teaspoon sea salt flakes

1 lemon wedge (optional)

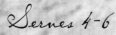

Serves 4–6

Rub the garlic cloves around the base and sides of each salad plate or bowl.

Wash and shake dry the salad leaves, then cover and chill. Tear them and use some of each type to line the plates or bowls. Scatter in some spring onions/scallions.

Break the tuna into coarse chunks and place on the lettuce. Rinse and dry the anchovies if very salty, then arrange in a criss-cross pattern on the tuna. Add the olives, eggs and basil. Dot the salad with the broad/fava beans, tomatoes, cucumber, artichokes and radishes.

Whisk together the oil and the salt, adding the juice from the lemon wedge (if using).

Drizzle this dressing over the salad just before serving.

A restored chateau

Surrounded by vineyards, orchards and lavender fields, Gignac
is an ancient hilltop village in the beautiful regional park
known as the Luberon, after its three mountain ranges of the
same name. This is superb walking country, especially because
of its proximity to Le Colorado Provençal, an area of ochre
cliffs recalling the extensive quarrying that began there in the
1870s and continued for more than a century.

ABOVE AND RIGHT

An unusual combination of grandeur and rusticity
characterizes the double-height entrance hall of
the chateau de Gignac. Apart from two iconic
pieces – a traditional curved-back settee and an
antique console table – the space is largely empty,
making it all the easier to appreciate the pattern
of the tactile cobblestone floor and the elegant
sweep of the staircase.

THIS PAGE The scullery is home to a
large collection of Provençal pottery –
all practical, working pieces that have
been well used over the decades – besides
linen and other items.
OPPOSITE The various pieces are
arranged against a backdrop of old
terracotta and stone. In the French
country kitchen, treasured objects are
displayed with a view to their aesthetic
qualities as well as to their accessibility.

Used mainly in the building industry for colouring plaster and cement, decorative tiles and roof tiles, natural ochre has now been largely replaced by synthetic substitutes, but the old quarry has been preserved for the enjoyment of visitors. Some 25 different shades of ochre can be seen from the hiking trails, ranging from the palest primrose to the deepest cherry red.

Occupying a dominant position in the village, on the site where a medieval castle once stood, is a fortified chateau built at the time of the French Revolution by a Provençal family called de Thomas. The events set in train by the revolution caused the Marquis de Thomas to flee, never to return, and the chateau fell into disrepair, remaining in this state until the end of the 1980s, when it was acquired by François and Michelle Joubert.

Every space in the chateau has since been renovated and restored in the most sympathetic fashion. A pair of wooden doors, tall enough to grace a barn, swings open to reveal a capacious entrance hall dominated by a broad stone staircase and a floor of worn and irregular cobblestones. Interior cobblestones are common in this style of house, and the Jouberts decided to emphasize their earthy tactility by

paring back the furniture in the hall to a minimum. On one side is a carved, painted and gilded console table beneath a large mirror. On the other side is a traditional three-seated bench known as a *radassié*. Apart from a few decorative objects, the rest of the space is empty.

This love of natural materials coupled with a minimalist approach to furnishings is evident throughout. When the Jouberts bought the house, there was nothing there. Every item was tracked down and purchased individually – at auctions, in antiques shops, at flea markets and *brocantes* – and all were chosen with great discrimination, resulting in a pleasing blend of old and new. The Jouberts were fortunate to live close to the town of L'Isle-sur-la-Sorgue, which, as well as hosting regular antiques fairs, includes nearly

300 permanent antiques dealers and second-hand shops – a fruitful source of furnishings for the chateau.

The main reception rooms are simple but elegant, featuring moulded plaster panels. The kitchen combines romantic elements, such as a classic refectory table and a well-used butcher's block, with more practical appliances, including a new cooking range, set into the old hearth. A collection of antique Provençal pottery is displayed against a backdrop of terracotta and stone in the former scullery.

On the upper floors are eight bedrooms decorated in subtle, muted tones, such as soft grey, duck-egg blue and pale rose, complemented by marble and terracotta floor tiles. Most of the rooms are enlivened with one or two dramatic pieces, such as a flamboyant chandelier or wall

THIS PAGE In an upper hall, pale grey walls are emphasized by a deeper dove grey in the alcoves and on the door panels. Offsetting the grey are plaster mouldings in bright creamy white. The grey-and-white marble-tiled floor anchors the rest of the scheme.

THIS PAGE A carved and gilded religious ornament resembling a sunburst adds a flamboyant touch to a simply decorated room. The drama is enhanced by the wall treatment. The area above bed level is finished with a yellow wash, while a terracotta band ties the lower part of the wall to the tiled floor.
OPPOSITE ABOVE The decorative surprise in this bedroom can be seen hanging above the fireplace, where a painting of horses at sunset and an antique mirror have been set into a painted and gilded frame.

hanging. In one room, an antique mirror and painting have been set into a painted and gilded frame; in another, a carved and gilded piece of religious ornament in the shape of a sunburst hangs over the bed.

A combination of old furniture, new plumbing and traditional-style fixtures gives the bathrooms an air of permanence. In another room, a long piece of furniture, possibly the base of an old dresser/hutch, has been converted into a modern basin unit, complete with plenty of storage space for towels and bathroom equipment.

ABOVE In a harmonious blend of new and old, a modern inset sink has been substituted for the original freestanding bowl in this antique washstand, which is paired with a traditional folding towel rail.
RIGHT To match the strength of the furniture in this bathroom, the walls have been painted a terracotta pink, providing a subtle background for the gilded mirror and the chunky wooden washstand with its decorative white china. The diaphanous curtain gives the room a subtle diffused light.

Foods from the wild

Vegetables, herbs and fruit dominate the flavours of the Provençal kitchen. In a region where the sun shines for almost nine months of the year, markets are usually overflowing with cultivated produce, but an extraordinary range of wild food is also available.

Wild spring greens are gathered from March to May. Some, including rocket, dandelion and purslane, go into the salad mixture called *mesclun*. Early spring is also the time for wild asparagus shoots, the top 20 cm (8 inches) of which are lightly cooked and added to egg dishes. Wild hop shoots and garlic leaves are abundant, and by late April nettles and sorrel are ready for spring soups.

In a region where the sun shines for nine months of the year, an extraordinary range of wild food is also available.

Huge numbers of culinary herbs flourish in the wild. Plants gathered from the high slopes or *garrigue* (heathland) are particularly valued. They include bay, mint, oregano, rosemary, thyme, winter savory and wild fennel.

June brings intensely sweet wild strawberries from the woods. Fruits such as bilberries and blueberries also grow in the wild, and early blackberries arrive at the end of August.

Autumn rains herald the start of the wild mushroom season. For collectors, the most prized mushrooms include ceps, milk caps and chanterelles. As the nights close in, chestnuts are roasted in open hearths, and in November the wild black truffle season begins. Called *rabasses* in much of Provence, truffles can be sliced wafer-thin and added to plain pasta dishes, risotto or buttery boiled potatoes. Alternatively, they can be poached and eaten whole, according to peasant tradition.

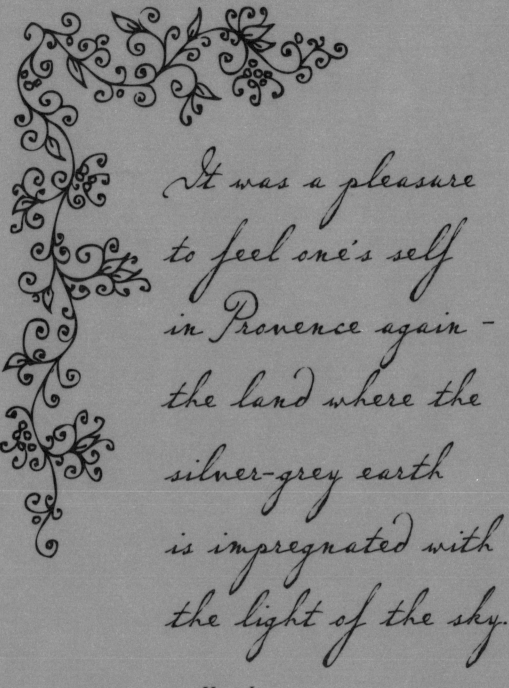

It was a pleasure
to feel one's self
in Provence again –
the land where the
silver-grey earth
is impregnated with
the light of the sky.

Henry James

to feel one's self
silver-grey earth
is impregnated with
the light of the sky.

Henry James

LEFT Old doors, many of them half-glazed, have been installed throughout the house. This one is arched in style.
BELOW The beautiful stone chimney piece is the star of the show in this part of the living room, but the basket of dried flowers, the bleached stone balls and the pile of coral add authenticity to the scene.
RIGHT The original exterior walls, dating from the 1950s, were made thicker and faced in local stone to give them a rugged appearance. Reclaimed shutters, painted soft sage green, open to reveal a gently arched doorway.

A perfect illusion

Not far from the Mediterranean coast, off the road between Mougins, famed haunt of artists and movie stars, and Grasse, perfume capital of the world, is a hidden treasure – an imposing stone house that appears to grow out of the rocky ledge on which it stands. Some of its features suggest that it may once have been a typical Provençal *mas*, or farmhouse, but nothing is what it seems.

LEFT The kitchen exudes a sense of permanence, giving the impression that it has always been there. This effect is achieved by great attention to detail. Even small items such as knives and forks are either old or designed in traditional fashion.

BELOW The kitchen sink is made of stone, with a copper tap/faucet that seems to grow out of the wall. As elsewhere, the walls are covered in a decorative finish called marmorino, which creates a wonderful softness and depth.

Indeed, when Isabelle Schouten and her husband discovered the property at the turn of the millennium, all it had to recommend it were stupendous views over wooded hillsides and olive groves to the distant ocean. The house then standing on this spot had been built in the 1950s with little concern for aesthetics. Their bold dream was to transform it into an elegant country home in the style of the 18th century, using authentic fixtures and fittings of the period, from the shutters to the bedroom cupboards.

It would probably have been easier to pull down the original building and start again, but the owners were more ambitious than that. Instead, they moved into a tiny cottage nearby and, with the help of an architect and a team of specialist craftsmen, set to work.

ABOVE LEFT This distinctive 'bubble' glassware from the nearby Biot factory has been made in the same way since 1956. Glasses, pitchers and vases are available in many different colours.

LEFT Kitchen storage shelves are concealed behind a set of old wooden doors with decorative diamond cutouts. The rustic table was found in a shop near the legendary antiques town of L'Isle-sur-la-Sorgue, near Avignon.

THIS PAGE Large tubs of dried flowers and other naturally inspired artefacts, teamed with an elaborate crystal chandelier, make a strong decorative statement. A distressed panelled door has become an artwork.

OPPOSITE All the elements of this living space have a beguiling air of authenticity, but everything comes from somewhere else. The paving stones, known as *barres de Montpellier*, were imported from Apt in the Luberon.

First, the outer walls of the existing house were made thicker and faced with the distinctive bleached stone of the area. The doorways and many of the windows were enlarged and given gently arched tops; glazing bars were installed at the windows; and a handsome 18th-century door found in the antiques town of L'Isle-sur-la-Sorgue was inserted into the front façade. Inside, the floors were covered with pale old flagstones known as *barres de Montpellier* and hefty antique chimney pieces were hauled into place.

Isabelle is a lifelong collector who relished the task of sourcing old building materials, windows, shutters, panelled doors, antique furnishings, kitchen equipment, lights, decorative accessories and all the other things required to turn back the clock on a house by 200 years. She was also keen to use on many of the walls the traditional marmorino finish, whereby ground marble dust is applied and polished, resulting in a soft, lustrous sheen.

ABOVE The antique cupboard door is in keeping with the timeless quality of this bedroom. A remnant of Indienne fabric was used to make the pelmet/valance.
OPPOSITE A colourful assortment of pillows and cushions and a couple of tactile linen throws add character to the master bedroom, where an empty picture frame above the bed introduces an element of mystery. A good way to use fragments of antique textiles is to make them into cushion covers.

When the work on the fabric of the house was complete, it was impossible to tell that it was not the ancient *mas* it so closely resembled. 'We love the irregularity,' says Isabelle. 'That sort of craftsmanship is something you just cannot find these days. These things are unique, a work of art.'

Now the rooms have an open and spacious feel, featuring carefully chosen period furniture. The central reception room is airy and cool with stone floors, a fireplace and sofas draped in antique textiles. As was customary in old farmhouses, the kitchen is dominated by a huge stone hearth and fireplace. An antique kitchen table is flanked by a smaller zinc work table and a row of cupboards, whose contents are hidden by a set of antique cabinet doors. Even the details, such as glass, china and cutlery/flatware, are either old or traditionally designed.

The upstairs rooms are large and full of light and, in keeping with tradition, there are few pieces of furniture in each bedroom. Colours are predominantly pale, textiles are old and patterns carry echoes of the past. Vintage linen sheets, sets of which are still relatively easy to find in the markets of southern France, add a touch of luxury to the beds, and toile de Jouy remnants have been used to make cushion covers and other decorative details.

Although Isabelle and her husband have succeeded triumphantly in creating an apparently authentic 18th-century-style home, the essential services — heating and plumbing, as well as kitchen equipment and electrical appliances — are entirely modern, for the whole idea was to make a house that was both delightful to look at and comfortable to live in. Now, more than a dozen years since work began, the house is everything that the couple could wish for. Among the finishing touches is a covered terrace leading from the kitchen — a traditional feature of the Provençal farmhouse — that makes an ideal spot from which to enjoy the views, while further terraces give structure to the lush hillside garden.

Sources

UK SOURCES

FRENCH ANTIQUES

Appley Hoare
9 Langton Street
London SW10 0JL
+44 (0)20 7351 5206
+44 (0)7901 675 050
www.appleyhoare.com
French country antiques.

Circus Antiques
60 Chamberlayne Road
London NW10 3JH
+44 (0)20 8968 8244
www.circusantiques.co.uk
Interesting antiques including many unusual French pieces.

Dix-Sept Antiques
17 Station Road
Framlingham
Suffolk IP13 9EA
+44 (0)7968 378 228
www.dixsept.co.uk
French, English and continental antiques and vintage furniture and objects.

The French House
41–43 Parsons Green Lane
London SW6 4HH
+44 (0)20 7371 7573
www.thefrenchhouse.co.uk
French antiques, lighting, fabrics and china.

Le Grenier
146 Bethnal Green Road
London E2 6DG
+44 (0)7720 890 393
www.le-grenier.com
Vintage French tableware, kitchenware and other collectables.

Josephine Ryan Antiques
17 Langton Street
London SW10 0JL
+44 (0)20 7352 5618
+44 (0)7973 336 149
www.josephineryanantiques.
co.uk
Chandeliers, antique mirrors, furniture and accessories.

Katharine Pole
+44 (0)7747 616 692
www.katharinepole.com
French antiques, decorative objects and antique textiles.

La Maison
107–108 Shoreditch High
  Street
London E1 6JN
+44 (0)20 7729 9646
www.atlamaison.com
Antique and reproduction beds as well as architectural items and bathroom fittings and some repro-duction pieces in the French style.

Pimpernel & Partners
596 King's Road
London SW6 2DX
+44 (0)20 7731 2448
Antique and vintage French furniture plus replica pieces.

Robert Young Antiques
68 Battersea Bridge Road
London SW11 3AG
+44 (0)20 7228 7847
www.robertyoungantiques.com
Vernacular French furniture and folk art.

Spencer Swaffer Antiques
30 High Street
Arundel
West Sussex BN18 9AB
+44 (0)1903 882132
www.spencerswaffer.com

FRENCH-STYLE TEXTILES & WALLPAPERS

Cabbages and Roses
www.cabbagesandroses.com
Romantic wallpapers and fabrics.

Elizabeth Baer Textiles
www.elizabethbaertextiles.com
French vintage textiles and haberdashery.

Jane Sacchi Linens
www.janesacchi.com
Antique linen and accessories.

Whaleys (Bradford) Ltd
+44 (0)1274 576718
www.whaleys-bradford.ltd.uk
Utility fabrics.

PAINTS & TILES

Farrow & Ball
www.farrow-ball.com
Paint in subtle, muted shades.

Limestone Gallery
+44 (0)20 7735 8555
www.limestonegallery.com
Limestone flooring and handmade French tiles.

Paint & Paper Library
www.paintlibrary.co.uk
Paint and wallpapers.

Papers and Paints
4 Park Walk
London SW10 0AD
+44 (0)20 7352 8626
www.papers-paints.co.uk
Historical paint colours.

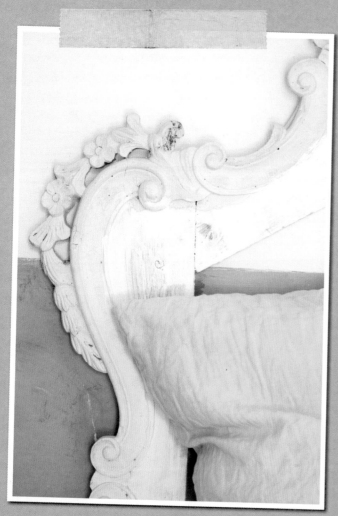

KITCHENS
Dibor
+44 (0)800 408 0660
www.dibor.co.uk
Tableware, linen and kitchen accessories.

Forneaux de France
+44 (0)1202 733011
www.lacanche.co.uk
Makers of Lacanche and Fornair range-style cookers.

The French House
50 Lamb's Conduit Street
London WC1N 3LH
+44 (0)20 7831 1111
www.thefrenchhouse.net
Well-crafted French kitchenware, plus lighting, garden furniture and textiles.

La Maison Bleue
www.lamaisonbleue.co.uk
French table and kitchen accessories.

Summerill & Bishop
100 Portland Road
London W11 4LQ
+44 (0) 20 7221 4566
www.summerillandbishop.com
Astier de Villatte ceramics and other beautiful and practical kitchen utensils, cookware, ceramics, glass, vintage linens and candles.

BATHROOMS
Catchpole & Rye
+44 (0)1233 840840
www.crye.co.uk
Antique and repro sanitaryware.

Stiffkey Bathrooms
+44 (0)1603 627850
www.stiffkeybathrooms.com
Antique sanitaryware.

The Water Monopoly
16–18 Lonsdale Road
London NW6 6RD
+44 (0)20 7624 2636
Fine French antique and reproduction bathrooms.

US SOURCES

FRENCH ANTIQUES
Elizabeth Street
209 Elizabeth Street
New York, NY 10012
+1 212 941 4800
www.elizabethstreetgallery.com
Architectural antiques.

Eron Johnson Antiques
www.eronjohnsonantiques.com
Denver, Colorado-based online retailer of fine antiques.

SALVAGE & RECLAMATION
Architectural Accents
2711 Piedmont Road NE
Atlanta, GA 30305
+1 404 266 8700
www.architecturalaccents.com
Antique fixtures.

Caravati's Inc.
104 East Second Street
Richmond, VA 23224
+1 804 232 4175
www.caravatis.com
Architectural salvage, including antique fireplace mantles, claw-foot tubs and reclaimed shutters.

The Preservation Station
1809 8th Avenue South
Nashville, TN 37203
+1 615 292 3595
www.thepreservationstation.com
Antique lighting, cast-iron mantels, and unusual architectural elements from all over Europe and the US.

TEXTILES & WALLPAPERS
Gracious Home
www.gracioushome.com
Bedding, linens and kitchenware, including Le Creuset cookware and French kitchen towels.

Scalamandré Silk, Inc.
979 Third Avenue
New York, NY 10022
+1 212 980 3888
www.scalamandre.com
Reproductions of classic fabrics.

Thibaut
+1 800 223 0704
www.thibautdesign.com
Classic, elegant textiles and wallpapers.

PAINTS & TILES
Country Floors
15 East Sixteenth Street
New York, NY 10003
+1 212 627 8300
www.countryfloors.com
Provençal-style ceramics, natural stone and terra cotta.

Janovic
East Side (at 67th Street)
1150 Third Avenue
New York, NY 10021
+1 212 772 1400
www.janovic.com
Quality paints.

Pratt & Lambert Paints
www.prattandlambert.com
Top-of-the-line paints.

KITCHENS & BATHROOMS
The Antique Hardware Store
19 Buckingham Plantation Drive
Bluffton, SC 29910
Unusual antique hardware.

Comptoir de Famille
www.frenchcountry-decor.com
Home accessories inspired by French country style.

Restoration Hardware
www.restorationhardware.com
Fine hardware, fine linen curtains, home furnishings, lighting, and other accessories.

Vintage Plumbing
9645 Sylvia Avenue
Northridge, CA 91324
+1 818 772 1721
www.vintageplumbing.com
Original bathroom antiques.

LIGHTING
Ann Morris Antiques
239 East Sixtieth Street
New York, NY 10022
+1 212 755 3308
www.annmorrisantiques.com
Reproduction lamps and shades.

GARDEN FURNITURE & ORNAMENTS
Authentic Provence
5600 South Dixie Highway
West Palm Beach
Florida, FL 33405
+1 561 805 9995
By appointment only
French garden antiques, planters, antique limestone floors, chandeliers, and furnishings.

Detroit Garden Works
1794 Pontiac Drive
Sylvan Lake, M1 48320
+1 248 335 8089
www.detroitgardenworks.com
French and English garden antiques.

Picture credits

1 Malcolm Gliksten's home in France. Photography by Claire Richardson; 2 The Chateau de Gignac, Michelle Joubert's home in Provence. Photography by Christopher Drake; 3 Hôtel Le Sénéchal, Ars en Ré, designed by Christophe Ducharme Architecte. Photography by Paul Massey; 4 The home of artist Claire Basler in France. Photography by Debi Treloar; 5 Photography by Debi Treloar; 6 Above left: photography by Peter Cassidy; Centre left and bottom left: photography by Tom Leighton; Above right: photography by Fritz von der Schulenburg; Below right: the home of artist Claire Basler in France. Photography by Debi Treloar; 8 Below left inset: the home of artist Claire Basler in France. Photography by Debi Treloar; Below right: photography by Tom Leighton; 9 Photography by Christopher Drake; 10–11 Photography by Alan Williams; 12 Photography by Peter Cassidy; 13 Above right: photography by William Lingwood; Below right: photography by Alan Williams; Below left: photography by Peter Cassidy; 14 inset below: photography by Richard Jung; 15 Inset: photography by Peter Cassidy; 16–17 The home of Virginie Denny, fashion designer, Alfonso Vallès, painter. Photography by Debi Treloar; 18–25 The home of artist Claire Basler in France. Photography by Debi Treloar; 26 Above: The Home of Charmaine and Paul Jack – Belvezet, France; Below left: Les Trois Salons, Uzes – Creators and owners Charmaine and Paul Jack; Below centre: Hans Blomquist and Frédérick Allouard-Rubin's home in France; Below right: Monte-Arena, Maison d'Hotes owned by Menelik Plojoux-Demierre and Patrick Buhler; All photography by Claire Richardson; 27 Above left: Chateau de Christin, Chambres d'Hotes de Luxe, Reception – Seminaires. Photography by Claire Richardson; Above right: Sharon and Paul Mrozinski's home in Bonnieux, France. www.marstonhouse.com. Photography by Debi Treloar; Below right: photography by Claire Richardson; 28 Inset: photography by Steve Painter; 29 Photography by Martin Brigdale; 30–35 The home of Marina Coriasco. Photography by Polly Wreford; 36 Bottom left: photography by Getty Images/Lonely Planet Images/Oliver Strewe; Above right: © Owen Franken/CORBIS; Below right: © John Lander Asiaimages/Alamy; 37 Photography by Education Images/ UIG/Getty Images; 38–43 www.franckdelmarcelle.com. Photography by Claire Richardson; 44 Photography by Steve Painter; 45 Photography by Martin Brigdale; 46 Photography by Steve Painter; 47 Above left, above right and below left: photography by Steve Painter; Above centre: photography by Kate Whitaker; Below centre: photography by Peter Cassidy; Below right: photography by Richard Jung; 48–55 The home of Virginie Denny, fashion designer, and Alfonso Vallès, painter. Photography by Debi Treloar; 68–75 Laurence and Yves Sabourets' house in Brittany. Photography by Jan Baldwin; 76 Above: photography by Richard Jung; Below: photography by Jean Cazals; 77 Background: photography by Richard Jung; Inset: photography by Debi Treloar; 78 Photography by Yuki Sugiura; 79 Photography by Martin Brigdale; 80–81 Annie-Camille Kuentzmann-Levet's house in Yvelines. Photography by

Christopher Drake; 82–87 Julie Prisca's house in Normandy. Photography by Christopher Drake; 88 Above: photography by Steve Painter; Below left and below right: photography by Richard Jung; Below centre: photography by Peter Cassidy; 89 Above left: photography by William Lingwood; Above right: photography by Richard Jung; Below right: photography by William Shaw; 91 Photography by Martin Brigdale; 92–93 Photography by Laurence Duris/Getty Imges; 94 All photography by Claire Richardson apart from above right by Debi Treloar; 96–97 Photography by Paul Massey; 98 Photography by Lisa Linder; 99 Photography by Martin Brigdale; 100–107 All items from Côté Jardin, Place du Marché, 17590 Ars en Ré. 0615886367. Photography by Paul Massey; 108 Above: Chateau de Christin, Chambres d'Hotes de Luxe, Reception – Seminaires. Photography by Claire Richardson; Centre: a family home near Aix-en-Provence with interior design by Daisy Simon. Photography by Christopher Drake; Below: owners of French Country Living, the Hill family home on the Cote d'Azur. Photography by Christopher Drake; 109 Above left: Florence and Pierre Pallardy, Domaine de la Baronnie, Saint-Martin de Ré. Photography by Christopher Drake; Above right: a country house near Mougins, Provence. Photography by Christopher Drake; Centre right and below right: The home of Jean-Louis Fages and Matthieu Ober in Nimes. Photography by Claire Richardson; Below left: Photography by Claire Richardson; 110–111 Photography by Kate Whitaker; 112–119 Mathilde Labrouche of Cote Pierre's home in Saintonge. Photography by Debi Treloar; 120–121 Photography by Alan Williams; 122 Photography by Richard Jung; 123 Photography by Martin Brigdale; 124–125 Photography by Jean Gill/Getty Images; 126 Background: photography by Martin Brigdale; Inset: photography by Richard Jung; 127 Left: photography by Peter Cassidy; Right: Chateau de Christin, Chambres d'Hotes de Luxe, Reception – Seminaires. Photography by Claire Richardson; 128 Photography by Martin Brigdale; 130–137 www.les-sardines.com. Photography by Claire Richardson; 138 Both left: the Home of Charmaine and Paul Jack – Belvezet, France. Photography by Claire Richardson; Right: www.franckdelmarcelle.com. Photography by Claire Richardson; 139 Below: Appley Hoare's 18th century converted Eau-de-Vie Factory in the South of France. Photography by Claire Richardson; Inset: the home of Bernard and Maxime Cassagnes in France. Photography by Claire Richardson; 141 Photography by Martin Brigdale; 142 Left and above right: photography by David Munns; Below right and centre right: photography by Richard Jung; 143 Photography by Richard Jung; 144–145 Photography by Claire Richardson; 146–151 The home of Jean-Louis Fages and Matthieu Ober in Nimes. Photography by Claire Richardson; 152 Photography by Peter Cassidy; 153 Photography by Steve Painter; 154 Above: The home of Jean-Louis Fages and Matthieu Ober in Nimes. Photography by Claire Richardson; Below right: Interior Designer Carole Oulhen. Photography by Christopher Drake; Below left and below centre: owners of La Cour Beaudeval Antiquities, Mireille and Jean Claude Lothon's house in Faverolles.

Photography by Christopher Drake; **155** Left: Hans Blomquist and Frédérick Allouard-Rubin's home in France. Photography by Claire Richardson; Right: Anna Bonde and artist Arne Tengblad's home in the Lubéron Valley, Provence. Photography by Christopher Drake; **156–157** Julian Elliott/Getty Images; **158** Far left: Maurizio Epifani, owner of L'oro dei Farlocchi; Photography by Christopher Drake; Left: photography by Peter Cassidy; Far right: Enrica Stabile's house in Le Thor, Provence. Photography by Christopher Drake; Right: Photography by Simon Upton; **159** Inset left: Maurizio Epifani, owner of L'oro dei Farlocchi; Inset right: Le Pavillon St Lambert in the Luberon Valley, designed by Blathnaid Behan of Behandesign. All photography by Christopher Drake; **160–169** Chateau de Christin, Chambres d'Hotes de Luxe, Reception – Seminaires. Photography by Claire Richardson; **170–171** Photography by Peter Cassidy; **172–177** Bruno et Michèle Viard: location–en–luberon.com. Photography by Polly Wreford; **178–179** Background: MOIRENC Camille/Getty Images; **178** Inset: photography by Steve Painter; **179** Inset above: 2012 Franco Origlia/Getty Images; Inset centre: Boston Thek Imagery/Getty Images; Inset below: photography by Tara Fisher; **180** Photography by Peter Cassidy; **181** Photography by Richard Jung; **182–189** The Chateau de Gignac, Michelle Joubert's home in Provence. Photography by Christopher Drake; **190** Above: photography by Richard Jung; Below left and below right: photography by Martin Brigdale; Below centre: photography by Peter Cassidy; **191** Above left: photography by Martin Brigdale; Above right: photography by Peter Cassidy; Below: photography by Simon Walton; **192–193** The Chateau de Gignac, Michelle Joubert's home in Provence. Photography by Christopher Drake; **194–201** A country house near Mougins, Provence. Photography by Christopher Drake; **202** Bruno et Michèle Viard: location-en-luberon.com. Photography by Polly Wreford; **205** Maurizio Epifani, owner of L'oro dei Farlocchi. Photography by Christopher Drake; **208** Hôtel Le Sénéchal, Ars en Ré, designed by Christophe Ducharme Architecte. Photography by Paul Massey; **Endpapers** Clockwise from bottom left: The home of artist Claire Basler in France. Photography by Debi Treloar; The home of artist Claire Basler in France. Photography by Debi Treloar; Photography by Tom Leighton; Photography by Tom Leighton; www.franckdelmarcelle.com. Photography by Claire Richardson; The home of Marina Coriasco. Photography by Polly Wreford; Photography by Tom Leighton; The home of artist Claire Basler in France. Photography by Debi Treloar; Clockwise from bottom left: The home of Marina Coriasco. Photography by Polly Wreford; The home of artist Claire Basler in France. Photography by Debi Treloar; Photography by Tom Leighton; www.chambres-provence.com. Photography by Claire Richardson; The home of artist Claire Basler in France. Photography by Debi Treloar; The home of Virginie Denny, fashion designer, and Alfonso Vallès, painter. Photography by Debi Treloar; The home of artist Claire Basler in France. Photography by Debi Treloar.

Acknowledgments

The author would like to thank all the owners who allowed us to photograph their beautiful houses and apartments. Many of them generously provided information about the restoration work involved in creating the homes of their dreams, including fascinating insights into the history of the buildings and their interior design and decoration.

Warm thanks are also due to everyone at Ryland Peters & Small responsible for the editing and design of this book, in particular Julia Charles, Annabel Morgan, Sonya Nathoo, Megan Smith and Maria Lee-Warren, and thanks also to Christina Borsi for location research.

Index

Page numbers in italics refer to illustrations

The French are the only people, except the Greeks, who have been at once philosophers, poets, orators, historians, painters, architects, sculptors and musicians .... And, in common life, they have, in a great measure, perfected that art, the most useful and agreeable of any, that of living, the art of society and conversation.

David Hume

The French are the only people, except the Greeks, who have been at once philosophers, poets, orators, historians, painters, architects, sculptors and musicians.... And, in common life, they have, in a great measure, perfected that art, the most useful and agreeable of any, l'Art de Vivre, the art of society and conversation.

David Hume